FILMMAKERS SERIES

edited by
ANTHONY SLIDE

The Films of
LENI RIEFENSTAHL

second edition

by
David B. Hinton

Filmmakers, No. 29

The Scarecrow Press, Inc.
Metuchen, N.J., & London
1991

British Library Cataloguing-in-Publication data available

Library of Congress Cataloging-in-Publication Data

Hinton, David B., 1950–
    The films of Leni Riefenstahl / by David Hinton. — 2nd ed.
        p.   cm. — (Filmmakers series ; no. 29)
    Includes bibliographical references and index.
    ISBN 0-8108-2505-8 (alk. paper)
        1. Riefenstahl, Leni—Criticism and interpretation.   I. Title.
    II. Series.
    PN1998.3.R54H56   1991
    791.43'0233'092—dc20   91-38996

To

Alexandra and Jefferson

CONTENTS

ACKNOWLEDGMENTS

For their assistance during my research for this book, my thanks and appreciation to: Leni Riefenstahl, who was graciously available for many hours of interviews and discussion, and for screenings and access to her private archives; Albert Speer, now deceased, but who provided my original introduction to Leni Riefenstahl and assisted through interviews and correspondence; Walter Traut, who supplied information on Leni Riefenstahl Film G.m.b.H.; the Deutsches Institut für Filmkunde in Wiesbaden, and in particular to Deputy Director Eberhard Spiess; Doris Rittgens and the Bundesarchiv in Koblenz; and the staff of the Berlin Document Center. My special thanks to Anthony Slide, who suggested and encouraged the second edition.

EDITOR'S FOREWORD

I recall my immediate and favorable response to David Hinton's study of the films of Leni Riefenstahl when it was first published by Scarecrow Press in 1978. I also remember my irritation at the negative reaction from the critics, an obvious reactionary bias towards a book which presented a sympathetic overview of the films of the director whom most scholars tend to study from a political rather than an artistic viewpoint. One film book reviewer, noted for never offering a bad review in his monthly survey of new titles, wrote what must surely have been his first negative comment when the Hinton book appeared. The book was scorned by the liberal establishment and soon went out of print.

Happily, a chance encounter with David Hinton at Vanderbilt University presented me with the opportunity to ask that he revise his original work for publication in the Filmmakers series. Cooper C. Graham's seminal study of Leni Riefenstahl's *Olympia* has already appeared in the series, and it seems more than appropriate to include this general overview of this extraordinary director's work.

Yes! Leni Riefenstahl *is* an extraordinary filmmaker. Without question, the greatest woman director of all time (although virtually ignored in feminist film circles), she is also one of the great pictorialists of the cinema, bringing to the documentary genre a style of filmmaking which uses visual images in much the same manner as did silent film directors such as Maurice Tourneur and Rex Ingram. *The Blue Light* has many obvious links to the pre-talkie era, as do, in more subtle fashion, *Triumph of the Will* and *Olympia*. The last two titles also clearly show that here is a master propagandist filmmaker—every bit as powerful in her use of material as was D. W. Griffith in the making of *The Birth of a Nation* or Sergei Eisenstein in the direction of *Potemkin*.

Of course, one cannot argue that Riefenstahl's propaganda is acceptable, but any student or scholar of the cinema must try and separate the propaganda from the art. And Leni Riefenstahl is a supreme artist of the cinema.

It has often puzzled me that a Soviet woman director, Esther Shub (1894–1949), whose career parallels that of Leni Riefenstahl—she directed films from 1927–1947—should all too often be praised and honored while her German counterpart is snubbed and vilified. Certainly, Leni Riefenstahl's career is closely linked to the rise to power and the monstrous years of Adolf Hitler and Nazi Germany. But Shub's career as an acknowledged Soviet artiste took place during the reign of another tyrant and mass murderer, Joseph Stalin. If Shub's career can be judged from a non-political viewpoint—and she certainly made many documentaries glorifying the Leninist era—then surely Leni Riefenstahl is deserving of the same treatment.

ANTHONY SLIDE

PREFACE TO THE SECOND EDITION

Time changes everything, sometimes glacially, sometimes with dizzying speed. When this book first appeared, the name Leni Riefenstahl was known only to dedicated cinemaphiles in the United States and Britain. In her own country, Germany, her status bordered on that of a "non-person," at least for the post-World War II generation. Since that time, the mass media discovered Leni Riefenstahl, fueled both by the increasing preoccupation worldwide with Hitler and Nazism, and also by Riefenstahl's own photo-anthropological work with the Nubas of the Sudan. Film journals, photography magazines, newsweeklies, and even *60 Minutes* profiled Leni Riefenstahl. The discovery inevitably prompted a reexamination of the woman and her works; voices raised themselves in defense of Riefenstahl's cinematic genius and, like this book, evaluated her aesthetics by her total work rather than just its most controversial work, *Triumph of the Will*. Almost immediately a backlash set in led by Susan Sontag's "Fascinating Fascism" essay, an articulate piece but with flawed scholarship, that did focus on her entire work but still through the distorting prism of the party rally film.

Preparing a second edition caused my own reexamination of Riefenstahl's work. My personal acquaintanceship with Riefenstahl gave me whatever advantage personal insights lend to critical works but also exposed me to justifiable questions of bias. The possibility that the enthusiasm for Riefenstahl's work evident in my writings might be more youthful exuberance than reasoned critical perspective haunted me as I started to read the text. After long deliberations enhanced by viewing the films again, that fear disappeared. The surfacing of certain facts in the intervening years necessitated some substantial revisions for the second edition, but the critical perspective remains the same. The lyrical beauty of her films enchants me now as much as ever.

The fact that the analysis that follows remains essentially unchanged in viewpoint does not mean that I am insensitive to some of the criticism that greeted its first publication. It was not my intention to dismiss the political implications of her work—remembering again that for most critics her work consists of one film, *Triumph of the Will*—but to ask for a separation of the film from the event so that the true political implications will be underscored and not dismissed. By focusing on the film instead of the event, critics overlook the monstrosity itself: the mass, symbolic manipulation of hundreds of thousands of participants at the Nuremberg rallies in so compelling and hypnotic a manner that film can only partially record. I do not believe, as one critic suggested, that Riefenstahl was unaware of the impact of certain shots in the film, particularly close-ups of faces in the crowd. Quite the contrary, she selected those shots precisely for their impact, attempting to approximate on film the induced hysteria reflected on those very faces in the crowd.

When I met Jesse Owens some time after publication of the first edition, he could hardly restrain his show of affection for Leni Riefenstahl. As a "star" of the film, he knew that *Olympia* is not, as described by one popular movie guidebook, a "glorification of the Nazi state," but an international celebration of athletic competition.

Hopefully, this book will continue to point critics toward a fairer examination of Riefenstahl's work.

DAVID B. HINTON
O'More College of Design
Franklin, Tennessee

CHAPTER I

THE BLUE LIGHT AND THE MOUNTAIN FILMS

Although Leni Riefenstahl's directorial career did not begin until 1931 with her first feature film, *The Blue Light,* she had already been in films for more than five years. She began her film career as the star actress in the films of Dr. Arnold Fanck, the founder of the "mountain film" genre so important to the German cinema during the 1920's and 1930's.

Forgotten today in his native Germany and neglected in most film histories, Dr. Fanck is nevertheless one of the most colorful figures in German film history. He was one of those early film pioneers who stumbled into the new art form rather than passionately seeking it out. His first film, *Das Wunder des Schneeschuhs* (The Miracle of Skiing) was made in 1919, and was nothing more than a skiing film with no pretense of a plot. At that time, Fanck had only seen one film in his life, and his passion was the mountains and not the cinema. When he sat down to edit his first film in his mother's kitchen, he suddenly realized that he had no idea of what to do or how to start. Fanck relates in his memoirs how he then decided to travel to Berlin with the intention of seeing as many films as possible, hoping to learn the secrets of the art of editing. But unfortunately for Fanck, instead of seeing a masterpiece of editing such as D. W. Griffith's *Intolerance,* he saw such films as Lubitsch's *Madame Dubarry (Passion)*, which he found too theatrical to be of help to him in assembling his all-action and no-theatrics skiing films.

Fanck finally learned editing the way most people do, through painstaking trial and error. When he had finished the editing of *The Miracle of Skiing,* he then discovered that none of the established distributors was interested in buying the film. At a time when German cinema was becoming world-famous with such expressionist classics as Wiene's *The Cabinet of Dr. Caligari,* no one was interested in the nature world of Dr. Fanck. Never one to accept defeat, Fanck proceeded to rent film theaters on his own and to attract his own audiences to prove the distributors wrong. The overwhelming success that he had in various German cities finally convinced the distributors that his films did have a public, and a buyer was found for his film. He continued to make more films in the same vein, first *Im Kampf mit dem Berge* (In Battle with a Mountain) and then *Eine Fuchsjagd auf Skiern durchs Engadin* (A Foxhunt on Skis through Engadin). Although each of these films broke box office records, Fanck slowly realized that the public would not continue to pay for films that merely recorded adventurous exploits in the mountains, and that if he wanted to keep his public, plots and dramatic structure would have to be added, no matter how simple.

For his next film, *Der Berg des Schicksals* (The Mountain of Destiny), Fanck used as the basis of his plot the true story of the first climbing of the Guglia di Brenta in Italy. A famous climber had attempted to scale the mountain, but failing after four attempts, left a tablet inscribed "This far but no further—no human feet will ever climb to the summit of Guglia di Brenta." Starting with this bit of real-life melodrama, Fanck enlarged the story by having the climber's son successfully climb the mountain in the course of a rescue expedition. It was only the barest of story lines, but obviously enough to enable Fanck to build an exciting action-adventure film around it.

In making these films, Dr. Fanck always remained an outsider to the rest of the German film industry. He wasn't interested in working in the huge studios of Neubabelsberg near Berlin; he only wanted to disappear again into the Alps to make his next film. In developing the mountain film genre, Fanck initiated one of the earliest realist movements in cinema history, and that is where his true importance lies. Primarily as a result of his experience in Berlin, Fanck believed that the cinema had to be different from the theater. Since his first concern was to capture on film the true beauty of nature, he had no use for studios, sets, make-up, or any of the other trappings of cinema that he regarded as theatrical and non-cinematic. He wanted his films to be realistic, and if he couldn't capture what he wanted shooting in nature, he wouldn't try to fool his audiences through artificial means. Although the demands of his increasingly dramatic films caused him to violate these principles on occasion, his striving for realism was often so intense and so successful that critics thought his nature shots were studio constructed.

Fanck also reacted against the unnatural, expressionistic school of acting predominant in so many German films of the day. He wanted natural movements, and his only concern for his actors was with their athletic abilities and how they performed from a distance, not with their acting abilities in close-up. In keeping with these beliefs, he employed amateur actors and complete unknowns. This principle would later be subverted as his repertoire company of amateurs became established professionals. If Fanck had been a film theoretician as well as a filmmaker, committing his thoughts to paper in the manner of Sergei Eisenstein, his beliefs would have made far more of an impact in German film history and he might have escaped the oblivion to which he is now consigned. Fanck's beliefs were intuitive and not part of an explicitly established theory of film, and Fanck was not the sort of person to spend hours writing about them at a desk. He remained a stranger to the film industry throughout his career, and when he stopped making mountain films and tried his luck in other genres, his creative career was over.

Fanck's films became steadily more dramatic and more successful, finally attracting the attention of Hollywood. After *The Mountain of Destiny,* Fanck made eight more films in the years 1925–1934.[1] The most famous of these was unquestionably *S.O.S. Eisberg* (S.O.S. Iceberg), the first film to be made on location in Greenland (with the assistance of the famous Arctic explorer Knud Rasmussen) and made in both German and American versions (with Tay Garnett directing the American version) for Universal.

But even though Fanck's historical importance is in developing and defining the "mountain film" genre, his importance for the rest of German cinema is not through his own films, but through his "discoveries"—the people he brought to film. Among those who owe their start in cinema to Dr. Fanck are Luis Trenker, who first acted in Fanck's films and later became a successful actor-director of his own mountain films; the cameraman Hans Schneeberger, who learned the techniques of camerawork from Fanck and went on to become the cameraman for Josef von Sternberg's famous *The Blue Angel;* Sepp Allgeier, the head cameraman for Leni Riefenstahl's *Triumph of the Will;* the cameraman Henry Jaworsky, who later worked for Riefenstahl and after the war went to America for a successful career in Hollywood; Hans Ertl, one of the major cameramen for Riefenstahl's *Olympia;* and of course, Leni Riefenstahl herself.

Unlike Fanck's own accidental entry into the world of film, Riefenstahl's was planned and deliberate, and totally indebted to Fanck. In her 1932 book on her experiences in Fanck's films, Riefenstahl tells the story:

> I stood tired and worn out on the platform, waiting for my train, which was already late. I had to clench my teeth, because the pain in my knee was starting to pierce again. Despite the pain, I tried not to think of the Doctor, who had ordered me to have an operation and a lengthy recuperation. I tried to forget my worries about the crack in my knee joint suffered in a dancing leap.
>
> I started to concentrate on the posters on the wall of the train station. Suddenly I became aware of a gigantic poster of powerful figures climbing a dangerous rock cliff. Underneath the picture were the words: "Berg des Schicksals (Mountain of Destiny) a film from the Dolomites by Dr. Arnold Fanck."

Just then I was tortured by the sad thought: what if I would never be able to dance again? And then suddenly I remembered that I had an appointment to keep, and here I was, standing hypnotized at this picture, at this towering rock cliff and the men who were climbing it.

I seemed to be waking from a dream when at the same moment the train departed and disappeared into the Kleiststrasse tunnel. But I did not regret that I had waited for nothing. The film in the poster was playing at the Nollendorf Theater at the other side of the square, and I decided to let the appointment take care of itself. A few minutes later I was sitting in the movie theater.

Beginning with the first shots, I was strangely affected by what I saw: mountains and clouds, alpine slopes and naked rock cliffs moved past me. I was looking at a strange and foreign world. Who would have thought that the mountains were so beautiful? I knew them only from postcards; they seemed lifeless and rigid, but yet they intoxicated me with their undreamt-of splendor. The longer the film ran, the more my excitement increased. The beauty and strength of the film attracted me so much that, even before the film was over, I had decided to visit the mountains and see them for myself.

Benumbed, agitated, and filled with a new desire, I left the movie theater. I was sleepless for most of the night, while I lay pondering if it was really the nature in the film that gripped me so much, or the artistic way in which the film was made.

Out of my dreams came reality, and a few weeks later I was standing for the first time at the foot of the mountains. After seeing the movie every evening for a week, I found that I could no longer endure to remain in Berlin. With joy I looked at the first rock cliff, wanting to hail it as a new friend, and greet it as an acquaintance. I sensed with a puzzling certainty that from now on, they would be a part of my life, and that they would have a special significance that I could then only vaguely begin to fathom.

I spent four weeks sightseeing, and then on the last day before my departure from Karersee, even in the last hours, I had a meeting that would change my destiny. I met Luis Trenker, the star of *Mountain of Destiny*. I spoke with him for a long time: long, hurried, and impatiently. "I am going to act with you in your next film," I told him. "Certainly, you can count on it," he laughed. He was at home in the mountains. He had grown up in them. "And mountain climbing?" he asked. "You can't climb? Such a young lady as you has no business being in the mountains," he said.

"I want to learn," I told him, "and I believe that I can do anything that I set my heart on." Even if Trenker had told me a hundred times, and had tried to prove it with all the manly logic that he could muster, that my chances to play in a Dr. Fanck film were next to nothing, it would not have made the slightest impression on me. I was convinced that no matter what, my dreams would be realized. With this in mind, I returned to Berlin. I got in touch immediately with Dr. Fanck, who had just arrived in Berlin to make arrangements for a new film. I telephoned him and mentioned Luis Trenker's name, and we arranged to meet in a cafe. It was remarkable how I was able to instantly recognize him, since we hadn't arranged any recognition signs. But I knew immediately that he must be Dr. Fanck.

With a racing heart I sat down and started to speak. My only wish was to tell Dr. Fanck what beauty he had created for me with his films. I talked and talked while Dr. Fanck sat quietly, stirring his coffee. I didn't have the slightest idea what kind of impression my enthusiastic words were making on him. Only once did he ask me a question. He wanted to know what my profession was. He knew nothing about dancing, nor was he acquainted with my work. Only when we were saying good-bye did he make a request. He asked me to send him pictures and critical reviews of my dances. And then I was alone again, standing on the Kurfürstendamm.

It was 7 o'clock in the evening, and suddenly I felt abandoned. It was as if a hard fist had shattered my dreams, and jolted me into the reality that my dreams could not come true. What had actually transpired? Nothing substantial. I hadn't even asked Dr. Fanck if I could act in his films, and he hadn't mentioned the possibility. He had only listened and asked who I was. But I was still determined, and felt that I was being pointed towards a specific future.

The pain in my knee started to return. I felt that today

my life had changed course and taken a different path, and because of this feeling, I decided to have the operation on my knee immediately. "A young lady like you mountain climbing?" Luis Trenker had teased. But he was more right than he could ever have imagined. With my knee in the condition that it was, I would never be able to mountain climb.

I went to the next telephone booth and tried to reach my Doctor. He was neither at the clinic nor at home. For months I had hesitated, but now I didn't want to put off the decision another moment. I must get healthy, so that I could go to the mountains. I got ready for the clinic, without even saying anything to my parents. Nor did I say anything to my friends. I wrote only to Dr. Fanck, because I had promised him the pictures and reviews. In the evening I entered the clinic. At eight o'clock the next morning I went under ether—and everything was forgotten.

On the fourth day a nurse came to me and announced a visitor. "Really, Nurse? Who knows I'm here?" To my surprise, Dr. Fanck had come to visit me.

"I brought something with me," he said, and handed me a sheath of papers. I unwrapped it slowly. It was a manuscript. The title page read: "Der Heilige Berg (The Holy Mountain), written for the dancer Leni Riefenstahl." What I felt at this moment, I cannot put into words. I wouldn't even want to try. I laughed and cried. I laughed for my luck, and cried for my bed-ridden illness. How is it possible, I asked myself, that such a burning desire can be so quickly and so completely fulfilled? A desire that I had never confided to anyone.

For three months I had to lay in casts; three immeasurably long months in which I did not know if I would ever be able to move my legs again. Dr. Fanck ran through scene after scene with me. With admirable confidence he sat next to me, never showing any doubt about the success of the operation.

In the thirteenth week I was finally allowed to stand. Eight days later the Doctor and Nurse helped me take my first steps. I discovered that I could move my knee again. I could walk again! Joy broke out over the Doctor's face.

Shortly before Christmas I had progressed enough to

be able to go to Freiburg, where Dr. Fanck had his own
studio and where he could make a screen test of me. I
applied my make-up, in large amounts. But a great load
was taken off my mind when Dr. Fanck declared that his
actors must do without make-up. He wanted a natural
appearance, not a film appearance.[2]

With these somewhat melodramatic events, Leni Riefenstahl was introduced to the mountain world of Dr. Fanck and
to the international world of the cinema. *The Holy Mountain*
not only marked the beginning of Riefenstahl's film career,
but a significant change in Fanck's films as well. For the first
time, the female presence entered his previously all-male
world and proved itself capable of performing the same feats
of strength as the males, despite the skepticism of Luis
Trenker. And the dancer motif of *The Holy Mountain,*
inspired by Riefenstahl, brought a more serious artistry to his
usually all-action films.

Today, it is impossible to see *The Holy Mountain* in any film
archive. Riefenstahl owns an old nitrate print of the film,
perhaps the last surviving copy in the world.

In *The Holy Mountain,* Leni Riefenstahl played the role of
a young dancer named Diotima, and, true to her prediction,
played opposite Luis Trenker. Her role employed the
dancing talents that she had exhibited on stages throughout
Europe before her knee injury, and she opens the film with a
prologue presentation of her famous "Dance of the Sea." It
was Fanck's intention to have the dancer symbolize the ocean,
and the male lead was to symbolize the mountains. This
double symbolism would supposedly contrast two of nature's
major elements, the mountains and the ocean, with man and
woman. The success of the symbolism is a matter of
conjecture.

As a project, however, *The Holy Mountain* appeared to be
cursed from the beginning. During her first day of skiing
lessons with Luis Trenker, Riefenstahl suffered a skiing
accident and broke both ankles. She was in casts for four
weeks. Hannes Schneider, a skiing champion playing one of

the male leads, slipped on ice and had to lay in traction for six months. The cameraman Hans Schneeberger had an accident in a quarry and fractured a rib. And another of the male leads, Ernst Petersen, tore a tendon in his foot. With that kind of luck, it is not difficult to see why it took Fanck two years to complete the film. It finally received its premier in Berlin in December of 1926.

Once she had recovered from her accident, Riefenstahl plunged into learning the tricks of mountaineering with all the enthusiasm that she was to exhibit later while learning filmmaking. Although Fanck had cast female parts in his films before, they were foils and never the equals of the males. But Riefenstahl quickly corrected the sexual prejudice as she proved herself capable of skiing and climbing as well as any of the males. It must be remembered that at that time, the Alps were not the well-developed resorts that they are today, complete with chair lifts, tramways, highways, and hotels. They were quite undeveloped, with only primitive overnight huts in most areas for those few who ventured to explore. Dr. Fanck's films, publicizing the beauties of the mountains for large numbers of people for the first time, including such city dwellers as Leni Riefenstahl, must be given partial credit for making the Alps the tourist attractions that they are today. Those who participated in the films with Dr. Fanck must also be credited with having admirable endurance levels, since the primitive conditions of the time had to be endured not only for days, but often for months, while they waited for suitable filming weather. With the erratic nature of alpine weather, the bright sunny days that Fanck needed were few and far between.

Riefenstahl's next role for Fanck was not as significant as her first tailor-made role. The film, *Der Grosse Sprung* (The Great Leap), was meant to be a skiing farce in the slapstick style of American comedies. It was also meant to be a slap at some of the critics who had been panning Fanck's films, including one, Roland Schacht, who dubbed Riefenstahl "diese ölige Ziege" (this oily goat) in one of his reviews.[3] The typically shaky Fanck plot concerned the adventures of "city slickers" in the unfamiliar terrain of the Alps, while the locals make fun of their inability to ski and navigate the mountains. The locals were played by members of Fanck's repertory company, with Luis Trenker playing the role of a peasant, cameraman Schneeberger leaving his camera to play the role of a skier, and Leni Riefenstahl, in a satirical reference to the Schacht review, playing a mountain goat herder. Exhibited in a country not exactly famous for slapstick comedies, *The Great Leap* was a commercial success.

The next Fanck film to feature Leni Riefenstahl was *Die Weisse Hölle vom Piz Palü* (The White Hell of Piz Palü). In the direction of this film, which contained an unusual amount of dramatic scenes for a Fanck film, Fanck was assisted by the famous German director G. W. Pabst, the director of *The Joyless Street* and *Westfront 1918,* among others. Pabst was engaged to direct those scenes in which emotion rather than action dominated, and which therefore required considerable dramatic skills from Fanck's athletic actors.

The opening of *The White Hell of Piz Palü* reveals that Fanck had mastered the art of editing, despite his initial handicaps in the area. The film opens with a young couple (honeymooners) climbing a glacier. There is a very rapid montage of the woman slipping and falling, while Johannes, the husband, tries unsuccessfully to stop the fall and save her. The quick montage and reaction shots of the husband's face are very reminiscent of the Odessa steps montage from Sergei Eisenstein's *Battleship Potemkin.* Following the death of his wife, whose body was never recovered from the glacier, Johannes remains in the mountains and lives the life of a crazed hermit, haunted by feelings of guilt over the accident. Years later, another young couple arrives on the same scene. This time it is Maria (played by Riefenstahl) and Heinz, her husband. Their idyllic honeymoon in a mountain hut is interrupted only by Ernst Udet (playing himself), the famous German flyer, flying over their hut to drop a bottle of champagne by parachute. But as shown in the opening sequence, the mountain is cursed for young couples, and later, while Maria and Heinz are climbing, they become trapped on an inaccessible ledge. Coincidentally, the crazed Johannes is also trapped there by the same avalanche. Nearby, the avalanche has buried a group of students who had also been exploring the mountain. A rescue party is formed by the village, and during their search they descend into a glacial crevice looking for the students' bodies. It is the same kind of crevice that claimed Johannes' wife. This scene is undoubtedly one of the most visually impressive scenes in Fanck's many films, and was actually filmed in the depths of a glacial cave using the light of the magnesium torches carried by the members of the rescue party. The combined effect of the lights, their reflection on the ice in the cave, and the smoke from the torches create an extremely eerie, while yet realistic, effect.

Meanwhile, newspaper headlines announce that the famous flyer, Ernst Udet, is on his way to search for his lost friends by air. After repeated aerial shots to show Udet's skill in flying through the mountains (before the film no one had ever had the idea to use airplanes in alpine search-and-rescue missions), Udet finally locates his missing friends on the isolated ledge, and signals their location to the rescue party by tilting his wings. But it is still a long time before they can be reached by the rescue party, and the three are forced to spend another freezing night on the ledge. Maria's husband has become delirious from exposure. In the night, it appears that he is freezing to death and in his delirium must be forcibly restrained. Johannes takes off his coat, which he had previously offered to Maria, and wraps it around the freezing Heinz. He then climbs to a higher ledge far above the young couple, curls up, and dies. Before he climbs to the ledge, however, he leaves a note, and the film ends with the rescue of the couple and the reading of the note. Heinz and Maria have been rescued, and Johannes has joined his wife in a frozen death.

Pabst was responsible for directing those few scenes that

were shot in a studio (a major Fanck concession) and the scenes on the ledge. But the action scenes of the rescue party, and particularly the descent into the glacier, were under Fanck's direction. Even though his films were short on plot, Fanck was a master at constructing action and building it to such dramatic crescendos that the audience was propelled along by the action alone. *The White Hell of Piz Palü* was certainly no exception to the Fanck style.

Furthermore, the engaging of Pabst to handle the dramatic scenes proved to be a wise decision, and the critics recognized Riefenstahl as a new dramatic actress instead of just another talented skier in Fanck's mountain films. A reviewer in *Close Up* wrote:

> Here, as never before, is the living spirit of the mountains, vivid, rare, terrifying and lovely. Other mountain films we have had, but we have never had *mountains*—almost personifiable, things of wild and free moods, forever changing. Nobody who loves the hills could fail to be held by this tribute to their splendor. . . . For the heroine, Leni Riefenstahl, renewed and unexpectedly fresh, unexpectedly charming. A flowing free rhythm, breath-catching beauty, genuine alarm. Not blatant or manufactured, but sensed with authenticity. The star remains the mountains. . . . [4]

Riefenstahl was now beginning to compete with the mountains for the public's attention.

With the completion of *The White Hell of Piz Palü,* Riefenstahl's career with the indefatigable Dr. Fanck was far from over, and three more films were to follow. The next was *Strürme über dem Montblanc* (Storm over Mont Blanc), the story of a lonely man's struggle with the wild elements of nature while manning a weather observatory at the top of the famous mountain. Made in 1930, it was Fanck's first sound film, and is sometimes known as *Avalanche.*[5] For this film, Fanck was innovative in his use of sound, particularly in having Bach and Beethoven beamed from the valley to the observatory station to relieve the monotony of the observer. The use of sound also proved that Riefenstahl, with a pleasant voice, would be able to make the transition from silent films to talkies without difficulty.

Besides his concentration on action, a definite pictorial style had also emerged in Fanck's films, one which would have a great impact on Riefenstahl's films. Fanck's favorite composition was low-angle shots of the mountain peaks with a backdrop of white, drifting clouds. Fanck wrote later in his memoirs:

> Now that there is color film, it is finally possible to make beautiful mountain films. But with black and white film, when everything was coated in gray tones, it was always difficult to distinguish the climbers from the rock face. Consequently, I almost always had to work in silhouettes, with the climbers framed against the sky or against a clear horizon.[6]

Thus, out of necessity, a pronounced stylistic device emerged which can be found throughout Fanck's films. The same kind of shots used for the climbers on the rock face, with clouds floating in the backdrop, were to be used later for shots of Hitler in *Triumph of the Will.*

The next Fanck film was another skiing comedy in the style of *The Great Leap,* entitled *Der Weisse Rausch* (The White Frenzy). For this film, Leni Riefenstahl played a different role; instead of playing a peasant goat shepherd, she played a spoiled "brat" from the city who has arrived in the mountains to learn skiing. Her instructor was played by the veteran Fanck actor Hannes Schneider, a European skiing champion before he started appearing in Fanck's films. Riefenstahl learns the art of skiing so well that she becomes a competitor of her instructor, and the film includes a race in which they are joined by fifty international skiing champions of the day. Comic scenes included a slapstick skiing race and a humorous portrayal of two "city slickers" ("Zimmerleute" in German) who are barely able to stand up on skis, played by the real-life skiing champions Guzzi Lantschner and Walter Riml. Both were later to serve as cameramen for Riefenstahl's *Olympia*.

The White Frenzy was a thoroughly improvised film, and was Fanck's last skiing film. He had intended to make the film from footage taken from his earlier film, *A Foxhunt on Skis through Engadin,* but he quickly discovered that film stock had changed too much in the intervening years and that he was unable to match the grains. This discovery necessitated a panicked search for new and additional financing, largely accounting for the improvisation in the film.

While working with Fanck, Riefenstahl was as eager to learn filmmaking as she was skiing and climbing. Fanck resisted the idea of teaching Riefenstahl the techniques of filmmaking, but through persistence and the help of Fanck's crew, she was able to absorb the art down to the smallest detail. In an interview, Riefenstahl described how:

> I soaked up Fanck's and his cameramen's experience until it became second nature. I needed no finder to know exactly which scene would require which focal length. I learned about over and underexposure effects and processing compensation. I got to know which lenses gave pinpoint sharp images and which affected sharp artistic results. Camera work became as interesting as using a paintbrush.[7]

As Riefenstahl learned filmmaking and started to consider the possibilities of the medium from her own aesthetic standpoint, she sensed that she and Fanck had two completely different personalities, ambitions, and approaches to the art. Riefenstahl found herself typecast as one of Fanck's mountain climbers, despite her critical dramatic success in *The White Hell of Piz Palü.* It was difficult for her to find roles besides Fanck's films, and her desire to enhance her career with better roles conflicted with Fanck's own ideas about the roles of actors and actresses. In 1928, while Fanck was making a documentary on the Winter Olympics (see Chapter III), Riefenstahl left Fanck to accept a role in a minor film entitled

Das Schicksal derer von Hapsburg (The Destiny of the House of Hapsburg). The film was a failure, and it did nothing to establish Riefenstahl's dramatic standing. Although she returned to Fanck, she realized that for him the mountains were always the star of the film and the actors and actresses would always be in the background.

But it was not only in Fanck's approach to dramatic roles that Riefenstahl found objections. As each Fanck film defined more and more the nature of the mountain film genre, she began to question his approach to the genre itself. As she commented later:

> Dr. Fanck had always made beautiful pictures, often with fairy-tale like qualities through the play of light, the snow, the ice, and the glittering results, but his plots were realistic. And I realized that for realistic plots, one should also have realistic, rather than fairy-tale like, visuals. That means, if a person wants to use such beautiful shots, then one should use a plot, either from fairy tales, legends, or ballads that are in agreement with the visuals. But when the plot concerns normal, realistic events, such as someone saving someone else, or someone flying, then the visuals should come out of real life as well. And with this feeling, that form and content should coincide, came the idea that I must write a ballad or a legend for such a film. That was the original idea. And for that reason I wrote *Das Blaue Licht* (The Blue Light). . . .[8]

While on a hiking tour through the Dolomites, Riefenstahl visited a village where she heard a legend that fascinated her. When she heard it, she realized that it was exactly what she had been looking for, and while its memory was still fresh in her mind, she returned to Berlin determined to make the legend into a film.

Her first step was to write a preliminary treatment, sketching in a rough form the plot and the characters. After the treatment was finished, she pondered her next step. Scriptwriting was not part of what she had learned from Fanck and his crew, and she admits today that writing dialogue is not one of her strengths. Finally, after showing the treatment to friends, she sent it to Béla Bálazs, a Hungarian film critic and theorist who at that time was considered to be one of the best scriptwriters in Berlin. She had never met Bálazs, but as a critic he had defended Fanck's mountain films against the attacks of other noted German critics, and was well acquainted with Riefenstahl's career. After reading the treatment, he became very enthusiastic about its potential and about Riefenstahl's own ideas for the film, and offered to help her write the script. Working in day and night sessions, Riefenstahl and Bálazs, along with additional assistance from Carl Mayer, Murnau's famous scriptwriter, finished the script for *The Blue Light*. It was 1931, and for Béla Bálazs, who was not only Jewish but a dedicated Marxist, it was to be one of his last major labors in Germany.

To make the film, Riefenstahl organized a small, independent production company under the sponsorship of Sokal Film, which had provided the financial backing for several of Fanck's efforts. Walter Traut joined her as production assistant and business manager, starting a long association that would continue through World War II and the making of *Tiefland*. Hans Schneeberger, who had left Fanck to serve as Josef von Sternberg's cameraman for *The Blue Angel*, agreed to be the cameraman, and Mathias Wieman signed on for the male lead, playing opposite Riefenstahl, who took for herself the lead role of Junta, the mountain girl.

The financing was sufficient to buy the needed film stock and rent the equipment, but little was left over. Everyone working on the film agreed to work without salaries, in return for compensation later when the film was distributed and earning money. Riefenstahl and Schneeberger made a four-week tour of the Sarntal and the Dolomites, searching for the locations. A small, quaint village in Tessin that perfectly fit Riefenstahl's conception of the village of Santa Maria was found. Its picturesque valley setting with a high mountain waterfall in the background was ideal for Riefenstahl's romantic, legendary story. The mountain Crozzon in the

Brenta-Dolomites was selected as the film's mysterious mountain. With the locations selected, filming began in the summer of 1931.

The Blue Light is the story of a mysterious light emanating from the summit of Mount Cristallo, which acts as a curse on the small village of Santa Maria at the foot of the mountain. Whenever the light of the full moon causes the blue light to appear, the young men of the village are lured to their deaths climbing the mountain in vain attempts to learn the secret of the light. Vigo, a young artist from Vienna, arrives in the village for his summer vacation, and despite the natural suspicion of the villagers, slowly learns about the curse that is plaguing the village. He makes the acquaintance of Junta, a young outcast from the village who lives alone in the mountains. She is shunned by the villagers and is regarded as a witch. When she appears in the village itself, she is chased and stoned. Following her through the mountains, Vigo falls in love with her and divides his time between her and the village. Later, when the blue light once again appears on Mount Cristallo, Vigo observes Junta climbing the mountain and follows her. He quickly realizes that Junta has discovered the secret that has so fatally eluded the villagers: the way to the summit and the source of the blue light. The effect is caused by the moon's light being reflected from a large cavern of beautiful crystals at the summit. Excited, he returns to the village and reveals his discovery. The next day the villagers follow Vigo to the summit, remove all the crystals from the cavern, and bring them to the village. Junta, walking in the valley, discovers a crystal that has accidentally been dropped and realizes what has happened. That night she attempts to climb the mountain again, but her treasured crystals, which had illuminated her previous ascents, are gone. She misses her footing and falls to her death. Her lifeless body is discovered by Vigo; in his attempt to help the village, he has killed his lover. The mysterious crystals of Mount Cristallo and the beautiful innocence of Junta, the mountain girl, have been lost forever by a misguided attempt to do right.

To bring her fairy tale legend to life while still retaining the unrealistic atmosphere she outlines earlier in this chapter, Riefenstahl pushed Fanck's techniques to their extreme. The film abounds with shots of mountain crags against a backdrop of drifting clouds, shots of Junta silhouetted against the sky, and quiet, pastoral shots. Maintaining another Fanck tradition, Riefenstahl insisted on doing all the difficult climbing scenes herself. When the script called for Junta to climb a sheer rock face without ropes, Riefenstahl did it on a mountain side without trying to duplicate the more dangerous feats in the safety of a studio set. She also persuaded Agfa, the film lab, to design a special film stock for her, which had a high green and red sensitivity and a low blue speed. The resulting effect was dreamy and romantic, cloaking the scenes with a light green effect. The stunning photography and strange atmospheric texture of the film contributed heavily to the film's popularity.

Although *The Blue Light* was a sound film, it was done in the style of early sound films, using sound only as an accompanying feature rather than as an integral element of the film. The dialogue is sparse, and, curiously enough, spoken in the Italian dialect of the region. Like Fanck's films, the plot is carried along by the interaction of the visuals rather than by the words spoken by the characters.

In a manner suggestive of Eisenstein, Riefenstahl has her camera study the faces of the villagers in close-up, characterizing their social situation as well as their feelings through a study of their faces. Like most of her stylistic devices, it was something that she would continue in the rest of her films. Instead of using professional actors, she employed villagers from the small village of Sarentino. It was no easy task to get them to perform before her cameras, since none of them had an idea of what a film was, and few of them had ever ventured beyond the secluded valley in which they were born. Riefenstahl's first attempts to even converse with them were silently rebuffed, so she rented a room in the village's small boarding house and spent days slowly making acquaintances in the village. She was determined to win their confidence, since their rugged, individualistic faces, which seemed to her to be right out of a Dürer etching, mirrored the right amount of suspicion and distrust for the villagers of Santa Maria. Slowly but surely the villagers came to trust her and finally agreed to do what she was asking.

When the shooting was finished, Riefenstahl then tackled the major task of editing. After making a rough cut, she was dissatisfied with her efforts and decided to consult Fanck for his advice. Fanck agreed to look at the film overnight. When Riefenstahl returned the next day, she found that Fanck had undone all of her editing splices and had taken the film completely apart. Three months of editing work was sitting on the floor of Fanck's editing room. Shocked and enraged, she threw the film strips into a laundry basket and took them home to start over again. But the experience proved to be beneficial. "This experience made me so critical toward my own work, that I ruthlessly left out everything that produced only length or monotony, no matter how much I liked the shot itself," she later observed.[9]

The Blue Light was a success at its premier in Berlin on March 24, 1932. The *Berliner Morgenpost* was particularly excited about the performance of the villagers, noting that "appearing as if carved out of hard wood, they give the film background and color."[10] The photography of Hans Schnee-berger was also applauded, although the credit must be shared with the director. *Close Up* was far less sympathetic in its review, and found the film to be straddling the fine line between art and *kitsch:*

> There are films which unfold before your eyes as a broad unit, each scene rising necessarily from the previous ones, directly mediating ideas and emotion. And there are others, where you feel the effort, the thought: I want to give you the impression of romance, of mystery, etc. *The Blue Light* belongs to the second group, you have no direct contact, nor the impression of genuineness.[11]

Instead of detracting from the film, this criticism only shows how successful Riefenstahl was in realizing her intentions of using reality to create a fantasy world, with the visuals complementing the legendary story.

Although *The Blue Light* is available today on videocassette, like so many other films it was difficult to view after its original release. Consequently, most criticism of the film is repetitive and unoriginal, merely echoing the conclusions of those few who had actually viewed and studied the film. Foremost among these sources is the film historian Siegfried Kracauer, who, although he admired the film's photography, contended that the entire mountain film genre was "symptomatic of an antirationalism on which the Nazis could capitalize."[12] This critical reasoning has been continued by the American critic Susan Sontag, who argues that *The Blue Light* and the other mountain films in which Riefenstahl acted form the first panel in "Riefenstahl's triptych of fascist visuals."[13]

To conclude that the mountain films were fascist in nature means to overlook the historical antecedents of the films, namely, the German Romantic movement, which revered the mountains as symbols of beauty and purity that were free from the corruptions of man. In his memoirs, Dr. Fanck acknowledged the Romantic origins of his work and lamented the death of Romanticism that now makes films like his impossible.[14] Many scenes in Fanck's films and in *The Blue Light* have the same composition and visual concerns of the famous paintings of German Romanticism, particularly those by Caspar David Friedrich. Despite the emphasis on montage in Fanck's films, there was a *mise-en-scene* that was definitely Romantic; and in *The Blue Light,* in which montage is supplanted by the Romantic *mise-en-scene,* Romanticism is brought to the screen with the full force that *The Cabinet of Dr. Caligari* gave to Expressionism.

Romantic aesthetics have little to do with Nazi ideology, and while some elements of Romanticism might have been adopted by the Nazis, it must be remembered that Naziism was a hybrid and wholly unoriginal ideology that borrowed

from everywhere, including Marxism. It was not the Romantic purity of nature that the Nazis admired, but the mystical,
dark and foreboding aspects that so perfectly complemented
Himmler's new Teutonic mythology. It was the vague and
mysterious outlines of the German forest, not the stark and
uplifting mountain peaks, that served as a symbol for Nazi
irrationalism.

Furthermore, to hold that mountain films were conducive
to Naziism disregards yet another important feature of the
genre that is a total rejection of one of Naziism's most
important tenets: the mountain films were decidedly anti-
nationalistic. Mountains are constantly depicted throughout
the genre as a unifying force that transcends national
boundaries. The action can just as easily take place in the
mountains and glaciers of Greenland (as it does in *S.O.S.
Iceburg*), the Italian Dolomites (as in *The Blue Light*), or the
Austrian Tyrol (in Luis Trenker's *Berge im Flammen*). Fanck
was even reprimanded by Goebbels for not making films that
took place in Germany. Italian, not German, is the spoken
language of *The Blue Light*. And in Trenker's *Berge im
Flammen*, love for the mountains causes old war enemies to
forget political differences and become friends through
mountain climbing.

Even with these similarities in the genre, it is worthwhile to
note the significance of the changes that Riefenstahl made in
the genre's formulas with *The Blue Light*. Fanck's films dealt
with the beauty of the mountains and the adventure of human
confrontation with nature. With his concentration on action
and adventure in a realistic setting, the psychological motivations of his characters were not explored. But in *The Blue
Light*, Riefenstahl not only shifted from Fanck's realistic
treatment of nature to a fantasized version; she introduced
the evil nature of humankind as a counterforce to the purity
of nature. The mysterious blue light that appears on the
mountain top is an idealized beauty; it becomes deadly only
because of human curiosity and greed. The mountain girl
Junta, as an outcast from the village, represents the pure,

trusting nature of humankind. The villagers are distrustful and hateful and persecute Junta because they do not understand her. Since the Nazis revered the villages as the cornerstone of their concept of the *Volksgemeinschaft,* Junta emerges as a rejection of that concept. Her purity is obtained not through living in society (or the *Volksgemeinschaft*), but through living outside it and away from its corruptions. Consequently, Junta is not the Savior or Messiah figure that Siegfried Kracauer always associates with Hitler in German films, but a martyr who suffers Christ-like persecution (rather than Hitlerian worship) by being stoned by a mob of the villagers. If there is a Hitler figure in the film, it is the Viennese painter (an interesting coincidence) who mistakenly believes that he is saving the village by removing the crystals, when the real result is to destroy one of nature's beauties and cause the death of Junta. In this sense, *The Blue Light* is a warning against Hitler, and not a preparation for him.

Another interesting critical approach to the study of *The Blue Light* and other mountain films is to compare them to another genre with similar concerns and styles, namely, the American western. As a genre, the western has much the same significance for the American cinema that the mountain films have for the German cinema. Further, both have distinct elements of composition that have a meaning of their own within the structure of the genre.

Both the mountain films and the western pit humans against nature as one of their central dramatic conflicts. In the mountain films, however, humans usually oppose nature for their own amusement (as in *The White Hell of Piz Palü, The White Frenzy,* and others), for recreation, or to prove something about themselves. In the western, it is humans against nature as a question of sheer survival. The mountain is there as something to be conquered; it is not a necessity of life that the mountain be scaled, only a fixation in the minds of those who attempt it. But in the western, nature (usually in the form of an intimidating desert) must be overcome in order for humans to survive or reach their destination. Thus, for the western, nature usually has a threatening aspect, as Peter Wollen discusses in his wilderness vs. garden thesis in his important critical study, *Signs and Meaning in the Cinema.*[15] Garden or wilderness, it is an inescapable part of life. This concept of nature is reversed in the mountain films, where nature assumes an idealistic and idyllic role. The mountains are a positive force attracting humans because of their beauty. If they cause death, it is not because of an intrinsically evil nature (as in the desert, which tries to claim its victims), but because of some error or default by the person involved, as in the accident at the beginning of *The White Hell of Piz Palü.*

The differences in pictorial composition are also significant. One of the most common shots of the western is the horizontally composed long shot of the vast horizon, particularly evident in John Ford's Monument Valley westerns. The standard shot of the mountain film, however, is vertically composed, a low angle shot looking up at the mountains peaks with clouds drifting behind them. The purpose of the horizontal composition in the western is to convey the immensity of the physical surroundings, while the vertical composition of the mountain films reflects the loftiness, both physically and spiritually, of the peaks.

In 1952, renewed interest in the film in Germany and Italy prompted Riefenstahl to change and reissue *The Blue Light.* Riefenstahl recut the film, added a new soundtrack, and then reissued it under the title *Die Hexe von Santa Maria* (The Witch of Santa Maria), reflecting the villagers' view of Junta. In the new soundtrack, Leni Riefenstahl and Mathias Wieman speak their old roles. A framing story was added to the film to make it more contemporary. The new version opens with a young couple arriving in an auto at a village. As they get out of their car before the village guest house, they are met by a young girl who shows them a crystal and a picture of a young mountain girl, later revealed to be Junta. Entering the guest house, they ask the proprietor about the young girl with the enchanting visage in the picture. Ordering his son to "bring the book," he begins to read a story from the book, and the original film begins. At the end of the film, when Junta dies, her face dissolves into the cover of the book, and the young lady in the framing story is seen looking into the waterfall.

Following the success of *The Blue Light*, Riefenstahl made one more film with Dr. Fanck, entitled *S.O.S. Eisberg* (S.O.S. Iceberg). Filmed on location in Greenland, *S.O.S. Iceberg* was Fanck's most ambitious film. It concerned a shipwrecked party on a floating but slowly melting iceberg, waiting to be rescued. The services of the pilot Ernst Udet were once again utilized, providing the film with stunning aerial footage of the Arctic never before seen in the cinema.

An American version of the film was made hand-in-hand with the German version, since the American studio, Universal, was providing the financial support for the film's production. The American version was directed by Tay Garnett and retained Riefenstahl as the leading actress. *The White Hell of Piz Palü* had been very successful in the United States, and Universal was anxious to cash in on Riefenstahl's new American popularity.

Riefenstahl later explained why she consented to make another film with Fanck after she had established her own reputation as a director:

> One of the reasons that I decided to go to Greenland and make the film with Dr. Fanck was that he was unable to find an actress to fill the main role, because he demanded too many athletic talents. And also, Universal requested that I act in it. The proposition was financially very interesting for me, because I was also to act in the American version. And further, it gave me the chance to visit Greenland, which at that time, had been seen by only a few people. I have never regretted my decision.[16]

Her career with Dr. Fanck had now drawn to a close, but Riefenstahl was now to embark on the part of her career that would make her internationally famous, secure her place in the history of world cinema, and change her life forever.

CHAPTER II

THE NUREMBERG TRILOGY

The Blue Light brought Leni Riefenstahl to the attention of not only the international film world, but to someone whose admiration for her work would far outweigh the opinions of critics: Adolf Hitler. Known to be an insatiable moviegoer, Hitler saw and admired *The Blue Light.* Always looking for proof of the "superiority" of German art, Hitler was undoubtedly aware that *The Blue Light* had won the Silver Medallion at the 1932 Biennale in Venice and was receiving critical claim abroad. Although it is probable that he was aware of her career in Fanck films long before he saw *The Blue Light,* their first meeting did not come until 1932. Hitler's introduction to Riefenstahl is described in the memoirs of Fritz Hanfstängl, an early supporter of Hitler.[1] The meeting seemed to have made an impression on Hitler, since he was to remember Riefenstahl after his ascent to power the following year.

Throughout her acting and early directing career, Riefenstahl appears to have been totally unaware of, and uninterested in, German political affairs. Her late childhood years and early twenties were devoted entirely to her chosen career of dancing, a profession demanding endless hours of practice and exercise which left little time for anything else, particularly political activities. After leaving dancing for the film world, she threw into her new career all the energy that she had previously devoted to dancing. Her total devotion to her artistic concerns made her an accomplished artist but left her ignorant of the outside world.

At the same time that Riefenstahl was spending months on

end in primitive mountain huts making films for Dr. Fanck, the Nazis were increasing their power in Germany. In 1933, they finally reached their goal with the appointment of Hitler as Chancellor. The Nuremberg Party Rally, which had been growing in size from year to year until it had become a gigantic extravaganza attracting hundreds of thousands of participants, assumed an additional importance in 1933. Under the theme "Sieg des Glaubens" (Victory of Faith), it was to celebrate the Nazis' coming to power. It was to be one of the most important gatherings in the history of the party.

Only a few days before the beginning of the 1933 rally (the rally was customarily held in early September), Riefenstahl was unexpectedly summoned to the Chancellery in Berlin for a meeting with Hitler. As soon as she was ushered into his office, Hitler asked her how her preparations for the party rally film were progressing. The question left Riefenstahl speechless. Although Hitler had ordered Goebbels' Propaganda Ministry to give the film commission to Riefenstahl, the Ministry had never informed Riefenstahl. The equally surprised Hitler then informed Riefenstahl that she must go immediately to Nuremberg and see if it was still possible to arrange filming on such short notice. The film was to be made under the direct auspices of the Nazi Party, with distribution by the Propaganda Ministry through government offices. Although the party already had its own film unit, Riefenstahl was given complete artistic freedom and was allowed to select her own crew.

With this strange beginning, Riefenstahl arrived in Nuremberg without any advance preparations to film a historical event that was to run for days and involve hundreds of thousands of participants at numerous locations scattered throughout the city. She was accompanied by three cameramen: Sepp Allgeier (Fanck's chief cameraman), Walter Frentz, and Franz Weimayr. The result of their hastily organized efforts was a short film, only 1700 meters in length, entitled *Sieg des Glaubens* (Victory of Faith). The title, like her two other party rally films to follow, was taken from the title of the rally.

The film disappeared in the destruction at the end of the war, and no copies have been discovered since. Riefenstahl's own opinion of the film is that it has little significance in her work, even though she does believe that under the circumstances, it was well-made. The main importance of *Victory of Faith* is that it introduced Riefenstahl to the unfamiliar documentary film form. For the first time, she was away from the organized shooting of a carefully scripted, planned feature film and confronted with filming events over which she had no control. The film also introduced her to the different editing style required for a documentary. To her surprise, she found that she took to the new form naturally.

Victory of Faith also marked the beginning of her long association with film composer Herbert Windt, who was to score most of her films.[2]

Following the completion of *Victory of Faith,* Hitler urged Riefenstahl to return the following year and make a feature-length film about the rally. Riefenstahl, however, was preoccupied with plans to make a film version of the opera by Eugen d'Albert, *Tiefland,* which had been a Berlin favorite in the 1920's. She was not interested in making another documentary and suggested that Walter Ruttmann, the maker of *Berlin—Symphonie einer Grossstadt* (Berlin—Symphony of a Great City), make the film instead. Ruttmann was a major film innovator and pioneer in editing concepts.

Her suggestion that Ruttmann make the film is indicative of Riefenstahl's lack of political sophistication at the time. Ruttmann was well known to have communist sympathies and was no friend of the Nazis. Riefenstahl was a good friend of Ruttmann but obviously had only concerned herself with his artistic beliefs and not his political philosophy. The same is true of her relationship with Béla Bálazs in *The Blue Light;* he, too was a very outspoken Marxist. Riefenstahl was an admirer of Ruttmann's kind of filmmaking, observing once, "What Fanck did with mountains, Ruttmann did with a city."[3]

Equally as strange as Riefenstahl's suggestion was Ruttmann's willingness to make the film. Despite his own political sympathies, Ruttmann was enthusiastic about making the film as a documentary of an important event. But Ruttmann's ideas went further than merely recording the event. He wanted to make the film a history of the Nazi movement, from its earliest days to the present, with the rally serving as a backdrop. Ruttmann proceeded with his plans, and Riefenstahl left for Spain to begin arrangements for the filming of *Tiefland*.

After the collapse of her *Tiefland* project (see Chapter IV), Riefenstahl returned to Germany in the middle of August, 1934. When she returned, she was informed by Rudolf Hess that Hitler had demanded that she, not Ruttmann, make the film. Ruttmann's ideas about a party history film did not appeal to the Nazi hierarchy, who were oddly reluctant to have films deal with this subject.[4] And furthermore, Hitler was anxious to have Riefenstahl expand on the work that she had begun with *Victory of Faith*.

What is known of Ruttmann's plans for *Triumph des Willens* (Triumph of the Will) reveal what the film would have been like had it been planned as a propaganda film rather than a documentary. Ruttmann's plan was to begin the film with a prologue which would dramatically reenact historical events from before the rally. The film was to open with shots of the frenzied German stock market in 1923, with rampant inflation driving stock prices to astronomical figures. The stock market scene would end with a trick shot of the market being flooded with a deluge of the worthless paper money of the Reich government. Then Ruttmann intended to show the other major event of 1923, Hitler's unsuccessful "Beer Hall Putsch" in Munich. The film would then be brought to the present with shots of Hitler in his airplane, on the way to the party rally in Nuremberg. A kaleidoscope of Nazi history would then be seen through Hitler's eyes, edited in the distinct Ruttmann style: the World War and the hated Versailles Treaty; unemployment and inflation, and scenes of economic misery; the unsuccessful Putsch and Hitler's imprisonment in Landsberg Prison; Hitler at his prison desk, writing *Mein Kampf;* the first copies of *Mein Kampf* rolling off the printing presses; and finally, the victory of the movement. With the victory, Hitler lands in Nuremberg.[5]

None of Ruttmann's footage survives, and it is not known how much he actually shot. But what he had filmed, Riefenstahl found unusable. As she described it:

> It was a chaos. He evoked the historical by use of headlines and such. You cannot create with paper in that way. The wind blew paper—poof! And the headlines were revealed. I couldn't use a meter.[6]

She did use Ruttmann's titles, however, for the film's opening. "I am not gifted at writing titles and dialogue," Riefenstahl notes. "I only do the visuals well."[7]

According to Riefenstahl, she met again with Hitler and agreed to take over the filming from Ruttmann if Hitler would agree to three conditions. First, that the funds for the film be arranged by her private company rather than by the Nazi Party. Second, that no one, not even Hitler or Goebbels, be allowed to see the film before it was finished. And third, that Hitler never ask her to make a third such film.[8] Hitler agreed to the conditions, and Riefenstahl left for Nuremberg to begin preparations for what would become another turning point in her career—the filming of *Triumph of the Will.*

At this point, several interesting questions emerge. The first: Why was Hitler so eager to have Riefenstahl make the film when the party already had its own film unit? The answer rests in Hitler's amateurish devotion to art (or at least his often misguided conception of it), a result of his own frustrated attempts at an artistic career in Vienna. Both Hitler and Goebbels had long hoped that the German cinema would produce a film to rival Eisenstein's *Battleship Potemkin* in artistic importance. And in Riefenstahl, Hitler saw the makings of a German cinema artist. Hitler did not trust the party film unit to create a work of art; they were useful at newsreels, but not cinema classics. Hitler and Goebbels often differed on the nature of Nazi propaganda; Hitler felt that politics and art should not be mixed, while Goebbels felt that the two could be subtly combined. Goebbels did not like the idea of inviting a party outsider to film the party rally, but the wishes of Hitler prevailed.

The second question concerns why Riefenstahl was so interested in keeping the film production separate from the party. The answer rests in the nature of Riefenstahl's relationship with Goebbels. Goebbels resented Riefenstahl not only for her unwillingness to join the Nazi Party, but because of his sexist attitudes toward women. Throughout her career, he constantly attempted to thwart the work of Riefenstahl, the only woman director in German cinema. Goebbels could countenance actresses in their stereotyped roles, but a woman director was too great a step for the propaganda minister. In addition, Goebbels, always jealous of his own power and personal position, resented Riefenstahl's access to Hitler and her ability to influence his decisions. During an interview with the author, Albert Speer commented on the intensity of Goebbels' animosity towards Riefenstahl and noted that Goebbels' opposition was known throughout the filming of *Triumph of the Will.*

If Riefenstahl was to consent to make another film under the direction of the Nazi Party and the Propaganda Ministry, she would risk the artistic freedom she enjoyed with her own production company. Also, from *The Blue Light* throughout the rest of her work in film, she preferred to work with her own production company rather than for studios and government agencies. The problem was settled through the creation of an "Abteilung Reichsparteitag Film, Leni Riefenstahl Film" (Party Rally Film Division, Leni Riefenstahl Film Company), a division of the company she had originally formed to make *The Blue Light.* Later, she followed the same procedure during World War II when her company made films for the German government.

Riefenstahl arranged for Ufa, the German studio giant, to provide the financing for the film. In return, Ufa had the distribution rights. Unlike *Victory of Faith,* which had been financed and distributed by the government, *Triumph of the Will* was produced along regular commercial lines.

Regardless of whether one accepts Riefenstahl's contention that the film is a documentary recording of an historic event, or, as some critics have charged, a deliberately conceived instrument of political propaganda, it is impossible to divorce the film from the historical events that occur in it. It is also impossible to understand the true importance of the film without understanding the historical background of these events. Provided with the necessary background information, certain sequences take on an added significance that would not otherwise be perceived during a viewing of the film.

The Nuremberg Party Rally of September 4–10, 1934, of which *Triumph of the Will* is the official document, occurred at a momentous time in the history of the Nazi movement. The importance of this period is emphasized in the opening of the film, with the only titles (done by Ruttmann) to appear in the film, thereby becoming the film's only explicit statement: "September 4, 1934. 20 years after the outbreak of World War I, 16 years after German woe and sorrow began, 19 months after the beginning of Germany's rebirth, Adolf Hitler flew again to Nuremberg to review the columns of his faithful followers."[9]

Only nineteen months since Hitler's ascent to power in Germany, his hold on that power was yet to be solidified. Two events which occurred before the rally had a decisive influence on what would happen at the rally. First, Hitler recognized the necessity of making peace with the German military before his grasp of power could be complete and secure. He was only too aware of what had happened before when he reached for power without the support of the military, ending in the disastrous suppression by the armed forces of his famous "Beer Hall Putsch" in Munich in 1923. Hitler's personal distrust of the German military, grounded in his dislike of the old German aristocracy which staffed the officer corps, was rivaled by the military's dislike of the Nazi S.A.[10] It was well known that Ernst Röhm, the commander of the S.A., envisaged the S.A. becoming the sole military force of the land, replacing the Wehrmacht and the German High Command.

To consolidate his power, Hitler was not above striking a deal with the Wehrmacht at the expense of his old party comrades in the S.A. On April 11, 1934, five months before the Party Rally in Nuremberg, Hitler met with leaders of the German armed forces on board the cruiser "Deutschland," and a pledge of support for Hitler was exchanged for a promise to eliminate Röhm, subordinate the S.A. to the army, and insure that the armed forces would remain the only military force in Germany.[11] The result of this agreement was the famous Röhm purge of June 30, 1934, only a little more than two months before the rally. Röhm and his top followers were assassinated in a wave of executions across the country, and Viktor Lutze, a previously unknown figure, was named to replace Röhm.

The second major event to influence the rally was the death of Reichspresident Otto von Hindenburg on August 2, 1934. Hindenburg's death allowed Hitler to consolidate the office of President, which had been held by Hindenburg, with that of Chancellor, already held by Hitler. With this move, Hitler became both the head of state and the leader of the government. Because of his previous pact with the military, there was no opposition to Hitler's consolidation of executive authority. Shots of military figures seen several times throughout *Triumph of the Will* indicate through their presence their support of Hitler and his party. In a hypocritical note, the rally itself was officially convened in memory of the recently departed Hindenburg, who had never been favorably regarded by the Nazis and who had been one of their major obstacles to power. It was not his memory but his death that the Nazis celebrated in their official eulogies.

With the army appeased and executive power now concentrated in Hitler's hands, the only possible threat to Hitler's power now lay within his own party. A purge on the scale of the Röhm purge could not help but have a major effect on the morale of the party, and no one knew what the aftermath might bring. With these events in mind, Hitler's address to the assembled members of the S.A., shown in *Triumph of the Will,* becomes a moment of great tension and high drama. William L. Shirer, an eyewitness, described the event:

> Hitler faced his S.A. stormtroopers today [September 9, 1934] for the first time since the bloody purge. In a harangue to fifty thousand of them, he "absolved" them from blame for the Röhm revolt. There was considerable tension in the stadium and I noticed that Hitler's own S.S. bodyguard was drawn up in front of him, separating him from the mass of brownshirts. We wondered if just one of those fifty thousand brownshirts wouldn't pull a revolver, but no one did. Viktor Lutze, Röhm's successor as Chief of the S.A., also spoke. He has a shrill, unpleasant voice, and the S.A. boys received him coolly, I thought.[12]

It is ironic that one of the film's most visually exciting sequences filmed largely from a specially constructed elevator behind Hitler's rostrum, becomes also an emotionally charged sequence in which Hitler's life was believed to be in danger from members of his own party. But all that is revealed in the film of Shirer's remarks is the presence of the S.S. guard separating Hitler from the brownshirts.

Understanding the historical background of the film is necessary when approaching the film as a document, but it reveals nothing of the nature of Leni Riefenstahl, the filmmaker. For that, the film itself must be studied apart from its historical background.

Riefenstahl insists that she used no prepared script for the filming of *Triumph of the Will* but relied on her own intuitive editing style. In interviews, she has been quite explicit about her approach:

> I didn't write a single page of text for either *Triumph of the Will* or *Olympia*. The moment I had a clear picture of the film in my head, the film was born. The structure of the whole imposed itself. It was purely intuitive. Starting from that idea, I sent the technical crew out on different tasks, but the true establishment of the form began with the editing.[13]

Despite its lack of written guidelines, *Triumph of the Will* lends itself to formal study. The film can be broken down into thirteen different sequences, with each sequence involving at least one event of the party rally, and sometimes more. This breakdown of sequences is not a purely arbitrary one; it is, rather, the manner in which the film divides itself, with the transitions between sequences discernible through the standard cinematic devices of fades and dissolves.

Though each sequence might be one event, that one event often consists of several parts. For example, the first sequence, "Hitler's Arrival," has two parts: Hitler's arrival by plane at the airport, and his parade from the airport to his Nuremberg hotel.

The thirteen sequences, with titles for later references, are:

I. HITLER'S ARRIVAL. Hitler's arrival at the airport and parade into Nuremberg.

II. HITLER'S SERENADE. On the night of Hitler's arrival, crowds wait outside his hotel window while a military band plays marching music.

III. THE CITY AWAKENING. An attempt to conjure the mood of the city of Nuremberg awakening in the morning. Also, a montage of scenes taken at the tent city which housed thousands of rally participants.

IV. THE FOLK PARADE. A folk parade, and an inspection of flag bearers by Hitler.

V. OPENING OF THE PARTY CONGRESS. Opening remarks by Rudolf Hess, and speech excerpts from other Nazi leaders.

VI. THE LABOR CORPS. A flag ceremony in honor of the dead of World War I, and a speech by Hitler to the Labor Corps, which is making its first appearance at a Nazi Rally.

VII. LUTZE ADDRESSES THE S.A. Viktor Lutze makes an evening address to the S.A.

VIII. THE HITLER YOUTH. Hitler addresses the Hitler Youth.

IX. REVIEW OF THE ARMY. Hitler and Göring review military maneuvers.

X. THE EVENING RALLY. The approach of the spotlit flags and a speech by Hitler.

XI. HITLER AND THE S.A. The memorial wreath ceremony, the advance of the flags, a speech by Hitler, and the consecration of the flags.

XII. THE PARADE. Hitler reviews a parade in front of the city hall of Nuremberg.

XIII. THE CLOSING. Entry of the party standards and Hitler's closing speech.

This sequential breakdown of the film facilitates the study of three of the most important aspects of the film. One is the actual chronological order of the events depicted in the film. Another is the relationship of the sequences to each other and with the overall editing pattern of the film. And the third is the internal editing pattern of each sequence, which can be approached independently as "mini-films."

One of the most common errors made about *Triumph of the Will* is the belief that the film is a straight, chronologically ordered record of the Party Rally. One critic has observed that:

> *Triumph of the Will* is structured straightforwardly enough, in the most literal documentary narrative tradition, events proceeding according to strict chronological order, starting with Hitler's arrival in Nuremberg, continuing through processions, rallies, and speeches in the order that they happened, and ending with the Führer's final address.[14]

By using source material available on the rally[15], it is possible to compare the construction of the film with the chronological order of the events during the rally. Table 1 shows the relationship of each of the thirteen sequences to the chronology of the rally. It reveals that *Triumph of the Will* is not "in the most literal documentary narrative tradition" but almost totally ignores chronological order in its structure.[16]

If actual documentary chronology was not Riefenstahl's guide in constructing the film, then what were her guidelines? Her own remarks provide the most accurate answer:

> If you ask me today what is most important in a documentary film, what makes one see and feel, I believe that I can say that there are two things. The first is the skeleton, the construction, briefly: the architecture. The architecture should have a very exact form. . . . The second is the sense of rhythm. . . . In *Triumph of the Will,* for example, I wanted to bring certain elements into the foreground and put others into the background. If all things are at the same level (because one has not known how to establish a hierarchy or chronology of forms) the film is doomed to failure from the start. There must be movement. Controlled movement of successive highlight and retreat, in both the architecture of the things filmed and in that of the film.[17]

Later, she becomes even more specific:

> I made everything work together in the rhythm. . . . I was able to establish that with the same material, edited differently, the film wouldn't have worked at all. If the slightest thing were changed, inverted, the effect would be lost. . . . There is first of all the plan (which is somehow the abstract, the precise of the construction); the rest is the melody. There are valleys, there are peaks. Some things have to be sunk down, some have to soar.[18]

This concept of highlight and retreat, peaks and valleys, can be applied perfectly to *Triumph of the Will* through observing

TABLE 1
Relationship of Film Sequence to Rally Chronology

Sequence No.	Event	Actual date of event (All dates 1934)
I.	Hitler's arrival	Sept. 4—afternoon
II.	Hitler's serenade	Sept. 4—evening
III.	City awakening	Sept. 7 or later
IV.	Folk parade	Date unknown
V.	Congress opening	Sept. 5—morning; also: Sept. 4, Sept. 5 (aft.), Sept. 6, Sept. 7, Sept. 8.
VI.	The Labor Corps Rally	Sept. 6—morning
VII.	Lutze addresses the S.A.	Date unknown
VIII.	Hitler Youth Rally	Sept. 8—afternoon
IX.	Review of the army	Sept. 10—afternoon
X.	Evening rally	Sept. 7—evening
XI.	Hitler addresses the S.A.	Sept. 9—morning
XII.	The parade	Sept. 9—late morning
XIII.	The closing rally	Sept. 10—exact time unknown, either morning or early evening

the arrangement of each sequence within the film. The film both begins and ends with a "peak," sequences of pronounced emotional excitement, and the highlights and retreats throughout the film are distinctive.

It had been Riefenstahl's original plan to begin the film with the "City Awakening" sequence. In her early editing experiments, however, she found that the sequence lacked sufficient dramatic power for a film opening. The sequence of Hitler's arrival in Nuremberg, which records the emotions of the crowds greeting Hitler, was substituted, and the "City Awakening" sequence was placed later in the film as one of the "valleys."

The first and last sequences, each of them a "peak," serve as a frame for the film. Because of the editing employed, the subject matter, and the complete domination of both sequences by Hitler, they are the strongest emotional and visual sequences of the film.

Throughout *Triumph of the Will,* sequences of high intensity are usually followed by more restrained sequences, creating a rhythmic pattern between the sequences.

An in-depth analysis of each sequence reveals even further how the film works:

Sequence I: Hitler's Arrival

If the viewer retains just one impression or distinct memory of *Triumph of the Will,* it will almost surely be the opening of this sequence. Almost all film history references to the film deal with this sequence, usually resurrecting Siegfried Kracauer's criticism of the mystical significance of Hitler's airborne arrival, which will be discussed later.

The film opens with Ruttmann's titles appearing on the screen to the accompaniment of heavy orchestral music, scored by Herbert Windt in true Wagnerian style. Riefenstahl made a wise decision to begin the film with the titles, since when combined with Windt's stirring music, they give the film a dramatic opening of their own.

The opening is a blank screen, and then suddenly a statue of an eagle appears, clutching a swastika—the symbol of the Nazi Reich. Large letters spell out the film's title: *Triumph des Willens.* The next frames reveal "Produced by order of the Führer . . . Directed by Leni Riefenstahl," and then continue with the Ruttmann titles.

Windt's music plays a key role in forming the audience response to the titles. Beginning with sorrowful, mournful notes that underline the message of the titles, "20 years after the outbreak of World War, 16 years after German woe and sorrow began," the character of the music changes to an uplifting, triumphant nature with the appearance of the title "19 months after the beginning of Germany's rebirth." This is the first indication of the important role to be played by Windt's music throughout the film.

After the titles, the mood changes again with the appearance of the visuals. The music becomes subdued, and shots of cloud banks taken from the air appear. The effect of these cloud shots is dreamy, and as some have suggested, mystical, because of the slow speed in which the viewer is transported. The cloud banks are of the steep and billowy kind perfect for such scenes. The audience is rarely aware that the shots are filmed from a plane.

In his book *From Caligari to Hitler,* Siegfried Kracauer compares a still of cloud formations taken from *Storm over Mont Blanc,* the Fanck film in which Riefenstahl acted, with a still of the cloud formations from *Triumph of the Will* to demonstrate that "emphasis on cloud conglomerations indicates the ultimate fusion of the mountain and the Hitler cult."[19] He also observes, "The opening sequence of *Triumph of the Will* shows Hitler's airplane flying towards Nuremberg through banks of marvelous clouds—a reincarnation of All-Father Odin, whom the ancient aryans heard raging with his hosts over the virgin forests."[20] This "Hitler arriving as a

God from the heavens" interpretation has become the standard critique of the opening sequence, unfortunately to the point of cliché. While the artist is not always capable of controlling the response of the audience to a film or what impressions the film might create, intended or not, it is certainly possible to say that Kracauer's reading of the sequence attributes to it far more symbolism than it deserves. As observed earlier, the cloud shots were standard stylistic devices of the mountain films, originated by Fanck and continued by Riefenstahl in *The Blue Light.* By the time of *Triumph of the Will,* this was already one of Riefenstahl's established compositional devices. It is not unusual to expect that she would use it in *Triumph of the Will,* particularly since she was striving to make the film on an artistic, stylized level rather than as a simple newsreel recording. *Olympia* also begins with the same traveling-through-the-air device in its prologue, with the audience being projected through the skies of Europe until a descent, similar to Hitler's descent to Nuremberg, is made into the Berlin Olympic Stadium.

In *Triumph of the Will,* the clouds suddenly part and the medieval city of Nuremberg appears below. With the appearance of the city, the accompanying music becomes "Das Horst Wessel Lied," the anthem of the Nazi Party. The complete plane is shown for the first time. Succeeding shots alternate between shots of the plane and of the city directly below, establishing a rhythm of shots. The shots of the city show long columns of troops marching through the streets below, re-emphasizing the titles "Adolf Hitler flew to Nuremberg again, to review the columns of his faithful followers." The shadow of the plane is seen reflected on the marching columns below.

Throughout this sequence, the editing pattern is highly visible. From the emergence of the plane to Hitler's entry into his hotel, the editing is a measured, rhythmical alternation of object-spectator, object-spectator, a one-to-one rhythm that flows throughout the sequence. The object is either the plane or Hitler, and the spectator is either a close-up of one particular member of the crowd or a shot of the crowd itself. As an example, the following is an abbreviated shot log of the first eight shots of the parade:

1. Parade starts, long shot (LS) of car leaving.
2. Medium shot (MS) of Hitler in car.
3. MS of crowd.
4. Close-up (CU) of Hitler.
5. MS of crowd (from left).
6. MS of Hitler (from behind).
7. MS of crowd (from right).
8. CU of Hitler.

This same rhythm was also used in alternating shots of the plane in the air with the city of Nuremberg below. The editing of this established rhythm is fast-paced throughout the sequence, with each shot being roughly the same length. The fast-paced editing adds to the emotional intensity already inherent in the sequence.

The camera point-of-view in this sequence is also noteworthy. The camera point-of-view makes this sequence unique, since it changes repeatedly between that of the camera and the subjective viewpoint of Hitler himself. Throughout the scene of the plane landing, the camera viewpoint is objective third person, recording both the spectators and Hitler. But with the beginning of the parade scene, the viewpoint suddenly shifts to that of Hitler. The parade is seen through the eyes of Hitler; the car passes under a bridge and the view looking up at the bridge is Hitler's viewpoint. The parade route is seen through Hitler's eyes, particularly when viewing non-human or inanimate objects, such as the tracking shots of a statue, a fountain, and a cat perched on a window ledge. They are the fleeting glimpses a person sees of an object while passing by.[21]

Just as in the editing, the selection of camera angles calls attention to itself. Every possible camera angle is used: aerial shots, eye-level, ground-level, and overhead shots. There is always movement as the camera tracks or pans the event.

Critics have often observed that the use of close-ups in the film is an insidious propaganda device. It has also been implied that these close-ups were staged to achieve the greatest effect. In reality, however, Riefenstahl used tele-photo lenses that were capable of putting one face in close-up out of a crowd at a distance of thirty to forty meters, allowing her to record unnoticed the emotional reactions of members of the crowd. The fanaticism evident on the faces was already there; it was not created for the film. The film merely recorded existing reality. The medium should not be judged guilty merely because of what it records.

Riefenstahl does use close-ups for more than cinema verité. At the end of the sequence, close-ups are used in a consciously artistic rather than documentary style. Here, they are of the S.S. bodyguard, lined up outside Hitler's hotel. In close-up study, their faces appear to be those of statues rather than living beings; they are reminiscent of the heroic faces found on the statutes of the favorite Nazi sculptor Arno Breker. Like a sculptor using clay, Riefenstahl molds reality on film until it becomes more than reality, a technique best described as "statues on film," which will not only recur throughout *Triumph of the Will* but will also become the major motif for the prologue of *Olympia*.

Another editing trait of Riefenstahl's already apparent is the technique of "dissection of detail." Following a shot of uniformed S.S. men standing in a row, there is a tracking close-up down the row with the S.S. men interlocking their hands on each other's belts to form a human chain. The close-up is of the hands gripping the belts. This attention to the details of an object, rather than to the object as a whole, is a Riefenstahl trademark. While the technique, thus ex-plained, might not seem very significant, it is one of the many artistic devices that separate *Triumph of the Will* from mere newsreel footage.

Sequence II: Hitler's Serenade

This sequence must be regarded as one of Riefenstahl's deliberate emotional valleys, following the emotional intensity of the previous sequence. A crowd is standing outside Hitler's hotel, waiting for a chance to see their Führer. Torches and spotlights are everywhere, and a band is playing martial music.

It is one of the scenes in which Riefenstahl utilized the aerial searchlights that had been requisitioned from the Luftwaffe for her use. At that time in the history of filming, techniques for shooting at night were still to be developed and refined, and Riefenstahl depended on these powerful searchlights to provide the lighting for her night shots. The light from the searchlights, many of which were directed upward into the sky, plus the light and smoke from the torches held by the crowd, lend an eerie effect to this sequence. It is very reminiscent of the spectacularly filmed scene in Fanck's *The White Hell of Piz Palü,* where the rescue party descends into a glacial crevice and the entire scene is filmed with the light from hand-held magnesium torches.

Sequence III: The City Awakening

A lyrical attempt to convey the feeling of the city of Nuremberg awakening in the morning, this sequence is heavily influenced by Ruttmann's *Berlin: Symphony of a Great City,* a film Riefenstahl admired. The sequence opens with a shot of church spires silhouetted against the dawn, then an indoor shot of a window being opened to show the city below, and a swastika flag unfurling in front of the window. The sequence continues with slow tracking shots of the city coordinated with equally slow and dreamy music, underlining the sleepiness of the dawn hours. To make known the time of day in a film that otherwise knows no time, there is a shot of church spires along with a bell striking seven on the soundtrack. Ruttmann used a clock face in similar fashion throughout *Berlin* to show the day's progression in time.

The rhythm of the "city awakening" shots is very slow, and the editing almost invisible. The tracking shots of the city are taken at the angle and speed of a person casually strolling along the sidewalk, and with the exception of a brief glimpse of a few human heads at the bottom of a frame, there is no human presence.

The sequence then changes mood, as aerial shots of a huge tent city are seen on the screen to the accompaniment of martial music, laughter, and voices on the sound track. Masses of people are seen on the ground, in contrast to the preceding city scenes. The tent city awakens and commences the morning chores.

Because of the preoccupation with what the film reveals of Naziism, an important feature of the film is often overlooked. *Triumph of the Will* is more than a document of the 1934 Nazi Party Rally; it is a document of the city of Nuremberg. The viewer is given a sense of the historic beauty of this medieval German city—an important contribution in view of the city's near total destruction in World War II. In several instances, the film rivals the so-called "city symphony" films in catching the atmosphere and flavor of a city at a given historical moment. In an interview, Riefenstahl revealed that when Hitler was trying to convince her to make the film, one of his selling points was based on his awareness of her interest in the old city, and particularly her fascination with the poetry of Heinrich von Kleist, Nuremberg's famous poet.[22]

Sequence IV: The Folk Parade

Lasting five minutes, this sequence contains no significant events. It involves a parade through Nuremberg of peasants in their native folk costumes, then ends with an inspection by

Hitler of a group of flag-bearers and Hitler's departure by auto.

The editing of this sequence differs from that of the first sequence because it lacks the central subject of Hitler around which to construct the editing. Without Hitler's presence for most of the sequence, the editing is slower-paced. Close-ups are used extensively to capture the flavor of the parade.

Following the folk parade, the folk music in the background changes to the Nazi anthem, the Horst Wessel Lied, and Hitler enters to inspect a group of flag-bearers. Close-ups of the flag-bearers follow, done in the same "statues on film" style used in the first sequence. In an excellent example of Riefenstahl's well-constructed editing, a shot of Hitler raising his hand in the "Heil" salute is followed immediately by a close-up of a flag-bearer jerking his head to attention.

Following the inspection, Hitler makes a grand exit by car. Succeeding shots show other Nazi leaders also departing in their chauffeured limousines: Rudolf Hess, S.A. Chief Lutze, Goebbels, and Hitler Youth leader Baldur von Schirach. Differences in the crowds and location indicate that the shots were not made at the same time or place, but were merely edited in at this point for no obvious reason.

Sequence V: Opening of the Party Congress

This sequence contains the first words to be spoken in the film, those of Rudolf Hess as he opens the party congress. In each of Riefenstahl's films, she deliberately delayed narration and dialogue for at least the first ten minutes of the film, establishing the dominance of the visuals. Besides Hess's opening, the sequence also contains a succession of edited excerpts from the speeches of other Nazi leaders.

Considerable confusion has arisen concerning the brief speech excerpts at the end of the sequence. Writing in his memoirs, Albert Speer, the architect and chief planner of the party rallies, noted that during Riefenstahl's 1935 party rally film (*Tag der Freiheit,* or "Day of Freedom"), certain footage was accidentally spoiled and was reshot in a studio reconstructed to look like the Kongresshalle, where the original footage was made.[23] The spoiled footage described by Speer sounded very much like the excerpted speeches in the 1934 *Triumph of the Will,* since Speer describes Hess, Streicher, and Rosenberg having to redeliver their lines. Speer also notes that Hess revealed true acting abilities when he was able to repeat his introduction of Hitler in the empty studio just as he had done in front of cheering thousands during the actual rally.

Riefenstahl, who was a close friend of Speer, challenges his memory on this point, noting first that Speer's date is wrong, and that the film was the 1934 *Triumph of the Will* and not the 1935 *Day of Freedom.* Furthermore, Riefenstahl states that only a short amount of footage of Julius Streicher was reenacted and refilmed, and not the flamboyant introduction by Hess that Speer described.[24]

According to Riefenstahl, all the speakers except Streicher were filmed during their actual appearances at the rally. But when Streicher gave his speech, the cameraman ran out of film and Riefenstahl was left without footage of the Nazi Gauleiter of Nuremberg, one of the most important men present. Realizing that she dare not leave Streicher out of the film, Riefenstahl decided to restage his address and had the Kongresshalle podium rebuilt in a Berlin studio. Streicher appeared, redelivered his lines, and the reshot footage was inserted into the film. It is an inconsequential addition, since the footage lasts for less than a minute in the film and cannot be seen as any different from the other excerpts.

But how could Speer make such a great mistake about the introduction by Hess? Riefenstahl's gentle correction of Speer is supported by other witnesses and photos in her private collection. During the preparation for filming in the Kongresshalle, Riefenstahl asked Hess to stand at the podium while she made adjustments in the footlights needed for filming indoors. Hess was asked to tell Riefenstahl when the heat of the lights became unbearable for a speaker at the podium, an important consideration when filming the fiery orations of the Nazi leaders. Hess took his assignment seriously and added his own dramatics. Riefenstahl recalls that Speer was present at that time and must have incorrectly concluded that she was filming the incident. Hence, the faulty recollection in his memoirs.

The opening shot of the sequence is a night shot of a flood-lit eagle grasping a swastika, one of the emblems used on the rally grounds. Since the opening of the Congress occurred during the morning, this shot must be regarded as a symbolic establishing shot having nothing to do with the events to follow. Riefenstahl chose to open several other sequences with similarly symbolic shots.

There is no discernible editing pattern in this sequence, which actually contributes little to the film and only demonstrates the fine line between art and tedium in documentary filmmaking. The speech excerpts are so short they are meaningless, and it has been suggested that their only purpose was to introduce the nation's new leaders to a pre-television society.[25]

Sequence VI: Introduction of the Labor Corps

This sequence presents one of the most difficult questions of the film. Although Riefenstahl denies that any of it was staged for her film, it presents some scenes that seem so obviously done for the camera, rather than for the crowd participating in the scene, that the appearance of staging, intended or not, is given. The dramatic devices used are interesting but detract from the documentary quality of the rest of the film: a "Sprechchor" for orchestrated crowd chants, a central narrator leading the Sprechchor, and well-orchestrated ordering and shouldering of spades and raising and lowering of flags.

The sequence opens with a close-up of the Labor Corps flag fluttering in the sky. The Labor Corps, Hitler's solution for the German unemployment problem, is making its first public appearance at this rally. Then follows a series of shots using the "dissection of detail" technique mentioned earlier. A medium shot of four Nazi standards against the sky is followed by a close-up of one of the standards. Not content with a mere parade of details and objects, Riefenstahl feels compelled to examine them more closely. With her, filming is more than a question of recording on film; the recording must be artistic. Another example in this sequence is a scene with the Labor Corpsmen standing in a row with their spades resting in front of them. A series of shots shows a close-up of the corpsmen's boots, then another close-up of hands folded on the spade handles, and then a medium shot of two rows of men with their ordered spades. The montage is typical of Riefenstahl's conscious attempts to establish a rhythm of editing.

Hitler is introduced to the Labor Corps by Konstantin Hierl, the leader of the Labor Corps, with the statement that "52,000 men are awaiting the orders of their Führer." As the figure is mentioned, there is a long shot of the crowd to stress the size of the crowd. Later, when Hitler makes reference to "millions of our comrades," the same device is used.

Following Hitler's introduction is a scene using the orchestrated narrator-respondent routine. With one very "Germanic"-looking young corpsman as the "narrator," the scene shows close-ups of the narrator standing within the ranks, asking of his other corpsmen, "Where do you come from, comrade?" A series of close-ups shows other corpsmen responding "From Silesia," "From Bavaria," and so on, until virtually every significant area of Germany has been named, indicating the national support of the Nazi movement. The gestures of the participants, and especially those of the over-enthusiastic narrator, are overdone and make the sequence one of the film's weakest.

Next, the Nazi slogan of "Ein Volk, Ein Führer, Ein Reich" (One people, one leader, one nation) is shouted by the crowd and illustrated by the film. The crowd chants "Ein Volk!" and there is an accompanying shot of a Labor Corpsman holding a flag, with columns of Labor Corpsmen standing behind him. Then "Ein Führer!" and a close-up of Hitler taken in the familiar low-angle against the sky style. And finally, "Ein Reich" along with a shot of a large mounted eagle clasping a swastika, indicating that the German state is now the Nazi state.

Suddenly a voice starts calling out the major battles of World War I, against a shot of a row of flagbearers. As each battle is called out, the flags are lowered even further until they touch the ground, visually symbolizing the disgrace of Germany with each defeat. The voice then cries out, "But you are not dead—you are still alive—in Germany!" and the flags are quickly raised into the air. The sequence concludes with Hitler's speech to the corps.

Sequence VII: Lutze Addresses the S.A.

The new S.A. chief, Viktor Lutze, addresses a night gathering of the S.A. Use is made again of magnesium torches and searchlights, making the sequence an interesting fusion of light, darkness, and smoke. Judging from Shirer's remarks about Lutze being coolly received by the S.A. men at the rally, it is interesting to note the end of this sequence, with Lutze's car being enthusiastically surrounded by S.A. men trying to shake his hand.

Sequence VIII: The Hitler Youth

This entire sequence is constructed around the person of Hitler, using his entrance, his speech, and his exit as the dramatic loci. It is the anticipation and then realization of Hitler's presence by the assembled thousands of Hitler Youth that gives the sequence its high emotional intensity.

As in so many other sequences, this one opens with a symbol, a close-up of the bell of a bugle playing a fanfare. Succeeding shots of members of the Hitler Youth pounding fiery cadences on drums set the tempo of the sequence. Even when he is not present, Hitler dominates the action, as the opening shots of Hitler Youth standing on their toes around the entrance reveal. As the crowd strains for a look, the noise level on the soundtrack increases and reaches its height with the appearance of Hitler. Riefenstahl is not merely a master of film editing but of sound mixing as well.

Shots of Hitler are always cross-cut with close-ups of members of the audience, taken with telephoto lenses. There are never two consecutive shots of Hitler in this sequence; each shot is cross-cut with a crowd close-up.

The sequence ends with Hitler's departure by car, with the crowd singing "Unsere Fahne flattert uns voran" (Our flag waves before us), the official Hitler Youth song written by their leader, Baldur von Schirach.

Sequence IX: Review of the Army

Although not the last of the film, the events in this sequence were among the last of the rally. The significance of the sequence is that it contains the only footage not taken by Riefenstahl's own camera crew. It shows army maneuvers performed under Hitler's watchful eye, and it was raining at the time. Riefenstahl later learned that the footage shot by her crew was completely spoiled and unusable, so she assembled this short sequence from footage taken at the same time by a Ufa newsreel crew. Considering the nature of the footage and its rather unexciting content, it is a wonder that Riefenstahl bothered to include it at all.

Sequence X: The Evening Rally

This sequence begins and ends with Nazi pageantry, from the entrance of thousands of flags in the beginning to the torchlight parade at the end. Searchlights are again used to illuminate the night action. The story behind this sequence is related by Albert Speer in his book, *Inside the Third Reich.* [26] The event is a rally of the "Amtswalter," the party bureaucrats whose overweight, middle-aged physiques did not fit Speer's carefully planned rally aesthetics. As a solution to their physical presence, Speer suggested having the "Amtswalter" march in at night carrying thousands of flags, thereby hiding their appearance. The searchlights were trained on the flags and on the great eagle which overlooked the podium. The cameramen were able to overcome the lighting handicaps, and the results are impressive as the flood of flags advance on the podium and the spotlit eagle.

Following the entrance of the "Amstwalter" and the flags, Hitler addresses the crowd. In a departure from previous editing style, there are no close-ups of anyone in this sequence but Hitler, obviously due to the inability to use telephoto lenses at night in an unlit crowd. This absence of inserted close-ups gives the sequence a unique aspect, however, since Hitler is the only human being seen. In previous sequences, while the crowd was faceless, it was nevertheless visible. But here people are so hidden by the thousands of flags that they are rendered faceless, literally as well as figuratively. While everyone else is hidden in flags and darkness, Hitler stands alone on the podium, bathed in the light of the searchlights.

Sequence XI: Hitler and the S.A.

This sequence can be divided into four sections: the wreath ceremony, the flag entry, Hitler's speech, and the flag "consecration."

An opening shot of a giant stone eagle and swastika dissolves to a long shot taken from the elevator which had been installed on one of the giant flagpoles behind the podium. The long shot is of Hitler, S.A. Chief Lutze, and S.S. Chief Himmler walking down the large empty aisle in the middle of the parade field, with thousands of S.A. men gathered on both sides of them. The soundtrack is noiseless, with only somber and muted music to establish the funereal mood. The long shot from the podium is replaced by a long shot from the opposite end, and the three men are seen approaching the columns of the War Memorial. They pause before a large wreath resting in front of the memorial. They bow their heads in silence, and the music stops. They salute, there is a quick insert of a swastika, and they turn and leave as the music resumes.

The composition of the above scene emphasizes the enormity of the Nuremberg rally. The men massed on the parade ground number in the tens of thousands, yet the scene owes its effectiveness to the three solitary figures walking in complete silence through their midst. It is a very moving scene and illustrates the flair for dramatics evident throughout the rally. The photographing of the scene also reveals Riefenstahl's uncanny ability to select the ideal camera location to capture the action in the most dramatic way possible. For this scene, the camera had to be apart from the crowd and the three figures; Riefenstahl's decision to build the elevator to film extremely high angle shots reflects her film background. In Fanck's films and in *The Blue Light,* it was always possible in the mountains to film from any elevation to obtain the best composition within the frame. In her elevated shots, low-angle shots, and use of elevators, firetruck ladders and rooftops, Riefenstahl was only applying a fundamental practice of the mountain films to the documentary.

Although Riefenstahl's fame rightfully rests on her ability as a film editor, her striking composition within the frame should not be overlooked. Her cameramen relate the zeal with which Riefenstahl would tell them how she wanted each scene filmed and from what location and what angle. By the time of *Triumph of the Will,* she had reached that state of mind that all film directors must someday reach, seeing the world in terms of the camera and the frame instead of through one's own eyes. Her ability to compose within the frame can be seen most strikingly in this sequence. Following the wreath scene, there is a parade of flags into the stadium similar to that in the previous scene, only more visible since it was filmed in broad daylight. There is one continuous shot in which the frame is filled completely with flags. Nothing can be seen but the flags, which move up, down, and forward as if they had lives of their own. Although something of the beauty of this composition can be seen in a still, its true beauty is revealed through the animation of the flags within the frame.

The sequence contains an important address by Hitler, during which he refers to the Röhm affair as "the shadow that spread over our party," and then absolves the assembled S.A. men of any responsibility for the shadow. As was done with the "Ein Volk, Ein Führer, Ein Reich" scene in the Labor Corps sequence, visuals are used to pictorialize Hitler's words. Hitler tells the crowd, "Our party stands like a rock," and the accompanying shot shows Hitler standing alone in the center of a massive stone podium. In the composition of the shot, Hitler appears to be a statue growing out of the rock of the podium. Taken together with the statement of Hess in the last sequence of the film, that "Hitler is the party, the party is Hitler," the allegory becomes obvious.

The final section of the sequence is the "consecration" of the flags, which Hitler performs by pressing the Nazi "blood flag" (the name given to the Nazi flag that was carried during the Beer Hall Putsch, during which several Nazis were killed) against other flags held by S.A. men. Often overlooked by film observers who are not familiar with Nazi mythology, this act was one of the many quasi-religious acts performed by the Nazis as party ideology became gradually elevated to religious status.

Sequence XII: The Parade

More than any other sequence, this is the filmed record of an event (the parade of September 9, 1934), and to film it, expansive and imaginative camera angles were employed. Given the monotony of a parade of uniformed men lasting over five hours, it was necessary to seek out as many different camera angles as possible to avoid transferring the monotony to the film itself. There are shots from rooftops and towers, from within the marching ranks, and shots that are framed in the window arcades of some of Nuremberg's oldest pieces of architecture.

The sequence begins with a low-angle tracking shot down a row of huge, unfurled flags along the parade route. Through the use of unusual camera angles, such as this low-angle shot, Riefenstahl calls the audience's attention to the beauty of detail which may not be observed by the unaided eye but which is accentuated through riveting the audience's attention to the frame. Her style is to go deeper into objects than any casual observer would; not content with the spectator's long shot, she explores the object closer, with a medium shot and finally a close-up. And sometimes the pattern is reversed, with surprising results. A shot shows a close-up of a hand outstretched in the Nazi salute. The camera pulls back, and the hand is revealed to be Hitler's.

Again, Riefenstahl's attempts to liven up a monotonous event yield pictorially pleasing results. With proper composition, a beauty can be created that exists only by virtue of its spatial relationships within the frame, a beauty not to be found in the unbounded reality outside of the frame. S.A. men march into an empty frame, with the combination of their ranks, columns, and projected shadows before them forming a striking pattern that gradually fills the frame as they march forward. Just as the artist composes within the limitation of the canvas, Riefenstahl composes within the frame and adds the extra dimension of film movement.

Sequence XIII: The Rally Closing

Consisting of two parts, the entry of the party standards and Hitler's speech, this sequence ranks with the first in establishing and reflecting high degrees of emotion and enthusiasm. Opening with a shot of an eagle and a swastika, it then shows Hitler entering the Kongresshalle to the accompaniment of cheers and martial music. Following Hitler's entrance, the party standards are paraded into the hall. The standards are patterned after those of Imperial Rome, with town names placed where the Roman standard read "S.P.Q.R." Two columns of standards proceed down the narrow aisle and then diverge at the location of the camera. The standards are shown in close-up when they reach the camera placement.

Hitler's speech is his last to the 1934 rally, and he uses a prepared text. While the other Hitler speeches in the film are more interesting from the standpoint of observing the reactions of the crowd (his speeches to the Labor Corps and the Hitler Youth), or in an examination of the speech's content (the speech to the S.A.), this speech is most important as a character study of Hitler himself. The cool, composed Hitler that has so far been seen throughout the film suddenly gives way to an intensely animated Hitler, whose excitement feeds on itself. His gestures become dramatic, interpretive flourishes and facial expressions those of a seasoned actor. The editing of the speech does a masterful job of conveying the mounting excitement of the event. The crowd's enthusiasm increases almost in direct proportion to Hitler's, and the alternation of shots shows this reciprocal relationship between Hitler and the crowd. Whenever Hitler makes a point that arouses a great cheer from the audience, there is always a cut to the audience. At one point the enthusiasm and shouting of "Sieg Heil" becomes so great that Hitler cannot continue, and the camera trains itself on the agitated Hitler waiting to resume speaking.

In several instances, the editing becomes very expressive.

Hitler asserts, "This racially best of the German nation demanded to be the leaders of the country and the people," and the statement ends with a cut to Julius Streicher, the party's leading racist nodding his head in agreement. Hitler refers to the "old fighters" of the party, and the statement is followed with shots of Hess, Goebbels, and Goering, the leading "old fighters" of the party.

Both the sequence and the film end on a mystical note. There is a long shot of the hall, showing the crowd and the standards. The crowd begins singing "The Horst Wessel Lied" and the standards are raised, appropriately enough since the actual title of the song is "Die Fahne Hoch" (Raise the flags). Then there is a long tilting shot upward to a large swastika on the wall, and a close-up reveals marching S.A. men superimposed on the swastika. The shot is a low angle one showing the marchers against a cloud backdrop. The film that began with Hitler coming from the clouds ends with the men of the S.A. marching into them.

Much has been said about the making of the film, and most of what has been said is incorrect. Errors range from the number of cameramen used to the extent of the preparations made for the film in conjunction with the planning of the rally. Some of the errors are insignificant historical mistakes; it is of little real consequence whether thirty cameramen were used[27] or 18, which was actually the case.[28] But the question of advance preparations made for the film, and their effect on the rally itself, is a question of crucial critical importance.

In his book *From Caligari to Hitler,* Siegfried Kracauer says:

> . . . the Convention was planned not only as a spectacular mass meeting, but also as spectacular film propaganda. Leni Riefenstahl praises the readiness with which Nazi leaders facilitated her task. Aspects open here as confusing as the series of reflected images in a mirror maze: from the real life of the people was built up a fake reality that was passed off as the genuine one; but this bastard reality, instead of being an end in itself, merely served as the set dressing for a film that was then

to assume the character of an authentic documentary. *Triumph of the Will* is undoubtedly the film of the Reich's Party Convention; however, the Convention itself had also been staged to produce *Triumph of the Will,* for the purpose of resurrecting the ecstasy of the people through it.[29]

It is this critical observation by Kracauer that has repeatedly damaged the film's reputation as a documentary, yet the observation is riddled with inaccuracies and mistaken conclusions based on faulty facts.

First, there is the historical fact that Riefenstahl did not arrive in Nuremberg until approximately two weeks before the rally began. With such timing, it is difficult to say that the rally was planned with the film in mind. Kracauer's reference to Riefenstahl praising the cooperation of Nazi leaders for "facilitating her task" actually refers to the thanks Riefenstahl gave to those who helped her after her arrival in Nuremberg for making arrangements for the quartering of her camera teams and other trivial matters hardly worthy of the importance Kracauer attaches to them. The book Kracauer refers to at other points in his criticism (*Hinter den Kulissen des Reichsparteitag Films,* which credits Riefenstahl as its author) is full of references to the difficulties she encountered in making the film, difficulties which would never have arisen if there had been careful advance planning. For example, it was difficult for speeches in the hall to be recorded, since only one row was made available for the sound equipment.[30] Other references are made to film towers that were not completed until halfway through the rally.[31] For many overhead shots, cameramen had to balance themselves precariously on the rooftops of the old houses of Nuremberg. There were other, more serious difficulties that were not reported. When Riefenstahl tried to engage one of Berlin's major cameramen to work on the film, he refused to work with her. When pressed for a reason, he stated that he "would not work under the direction of a women."[32]

There are other reasons to doubt Kracauer's critical

premises. His argument is supported by only one sentence taken from the Riefenstahl book: "The preparations for the Party Convention were made in concert with the preparations for the camera work." This one sentence is not taken from the body of the text but from a caption for a photo, and photo captions, since they are usually tailored to fit the photo, are notoriously unreliable sources of information. There is the additional fact that since Kracauer wrote his criticism, it has been learned that Riefenstahl did not actually write her book. It was ghostwritten for her by Ernest Jäger, a German film magazine editor who had been commissioned by the publicity department of Ufa.[33]

An even more substantial question must be posed: is it really logical to presume that the rally, and the architecture designed for it, would have been any different without the presence of Riefenstahl and her camera crews? The history of the Nuremberg rallies indicates that, even though their filmic value was later appreciated, the rally was the central event of the party and was staged for the benefit of those hundreds of thousands actually in attendance. The film could only attempt to show the fanaticism that was evident at the rally; that Riefenstahl was able to capture these feelings on film as effectively as she did, particularly through her use of the telephoto lens to record reactions unnoticed, is a tribute to her abilities as a documentary filmmaker.

Also, it is not logical to presume that Albert Speer, the architect of the rally, would have altered his architectural plans for the one-shot benefit of Riefenstahl and her film crew. Riefenstahl filmed just one rally in its entirety, while the buildings were designed to stand for centuries. Speer's own memoirs point out that the *raison d'être* of Nazi architecture was quite independent of its cinematic possibilities.

As a final comment on the question, Speer denied in an interview with the author that the film and the rally were planned hand-in-hand. Terming Kracauer's statements "nonsense," Speer noted that whenever he was approached to make an alteration or change in his plans in order to accommodate the film, he strenuously opposed it, since it might either change the harmony of his architecture or alter his central plans for the rally. He stated that he consented to only the slightest concessions for the filming, such as allowing more room on a platform for a camera, which were of such a trivial nature that they did not actually constitute concessions. The only notable concession that he did agree to was the placing of an elevator on the giant flag pole so that Riefenstahl could obtain the overhead shots that she desired, and even that concession was arranged only shortly before the beginning of the rally.

Even today, more than fifty years after the making of the film, the controversy continues.

The only thing conceded by all sides is the film's importance in film history; otherwise, critical opinion goes from one extreme to the other. The most dangerous error is to approach *Triumph of the Will* as either pure propaganda or pure documentary. It must be viewed as somewhere between the two. Perhaps the best definition of the film is that offered by Richard Corliss, who wrote that *Triumph of the Will* is "a sympathetic documentary of a propaganda event."[34]

There is no doubt that at the time of the making of the film, Leni Riefenstahl was attracted to Hitler and the Nazi movement. She has never denied that fact. *Triumph of the Will* was made at an early moment in the history of the Nazi rule: the notorious Nuremberg race laws had not yet been passed, and even countries that were later to become enemies of Germany were represented officially at the Nuremberg rally by ambassadors and diplomats. The most conclusive evidence on Riefenstahl's behalf is the Gold Medallion awarded *Triumph of the Will* at the Paris World Exhibition in 1937. Had the film been regarded as pure Nazi propaganda, it would never have received such an award just two years before the outbreak of World War II.

In her attempts to enrich the film artistically and avoid newsreel reportage, Riefenstahl often took steps that will forever be open to critical interpretation. An artist's true intentions can never be fully understood, not at the time, and not many years later. But a work can and should be examined against the maker's previous works in an attempt to ascertain whether certain features are established stylistic traits of the artist and if they have a significance that can only be determined through an examination of the artist's total work. In the case of Leni Riefenstahl, such an examination reveals that the cloud motif at the beginning of *Triumph of the Will* is more of a stylistic device inherited from the mountain-film genre than a specifically intended "Odin descending from the heavens" theme.

The third member of Riefenstahl's trilogy of films for the Nazis is the short film *Tag der Freiheit: Unser Wehrmacht* (Day of Freedom: Our Army). Like *Victory of Faith* and *Triumph of the Will* before it, the heroic-sounding title is taken from the name the Nazis gave the party rally of that year (1935).

According to Riefenstahl, she received bitter complaints from leaders of the German army after the filming of *Triumph of the Will*. The generals felt that the army had been overlooked in favor of the party throughout the film. Indeed, the army appears only in a short sequence of the film (Sequence IX—Review of the Army) and even then, as observed earlier, only in newsreel footage edited in by Riefenstahl.

The wrath of the generals was so great that they brought their case directly to Hitler, and the result was Riefenstahl's first disagreeable words with Hitler. At a meeting with Riefenstahl at Rudolf Hess's Munich home, Hitler attempted to suggest an "artistic" compromise to the problem. His proposal was that Riefenstahl line up all the overlooked generals in a row and then have the camera slowly track down the row so that each general would be seen in the film and his ego placated. To make matters worse, Hitler suggested that this shot be used as the opening of the film. Riefenstahl turned down both proposals immediately; the proposed shot was precisely the kind she had tried to avoid throughout the film, and besides, she had already decided on how she wanted to open the film. When she refused the proposals, Hitler looked at her very coldly, remarked, "You are very obstinate. I only wanted to help you," and left the room. But keeping his earlier promise to Riefenstahl, he made no further attempts to interfere with the film.

After this event, Riefenstahl resolved to try to soothe the ruffled feathers of the Wehrmacht generals. She agreed to return to the following party rally in 1935 and make a film exclusively about the Wehrmacht. She honored the promise and returned the next fall with six cameramen. Her heart was not in the project, though, and she was determined to make the film as quickly as possible. The film was financed by the party through Riefenstahl's own film company and was distributed to German theaters as a short by Ufa.

Day of Freedom was lost at the end of the war and remained lost until the mid-1970s when an incomplete print was discovered in the United States. It is an unexciting film, and the viewer can see immediately that Riefenstahl was only fulfilling a commitment and not trying to make a cinema classic. Only the very beginning of the film is worthy of note. It opens with a shot of marching soldiers, obviously filmed in a set, marching through foggy darkness. Then a distorted wall, done in true expressionistic style and reminiscent of the sets of *The Cabinet of Dr. Caligari,* is shown, with a soldier standing in front of two windows in the wall. The dark silhouette of the soldier is shown looming against the sky. This staging is a significant departure from Riefenstahl's documentary style in *Triumph of the Will* but is an indication of what is to come in the prologue of *Olympia,*

The rest of the film could have been taken directly from *Triumph of the Will.* As Riefenstahl herself admits, the style is identical. There is a sequence of a tent city awakening in the morning and people performing their morning chores, just as in *Triumph of the Will.* There are also numerous low-angle shots of marching soldiers framed against a backdrop of clouds. A soldier blowing a trumpet turns until the horn of the trumpet completely fills the frame (also as in *Triumph of the Will*); this is followed by a dissolve to the Speer-designed eagle, rows of swastika flags, and then a final settling on an iron cross flag, representing the Wehrmacht. One pan shot across a large stadium audience gives the only indication (in the surviving print) that the film was made at the party rally. The rest of the film is devoted to scenes of war maneuvers involving light artillery, machine guns, tanks, and smoke bombs, all performed under the watchful eye of Hitler. The final shot of the film shows planes flying overhead in a swastika formation, which is then superimposed on a swastika flag.

What survives of the film is of little interest after the accomplishments of *Triumph of the Will*. The central part of the film, which Riefenstahl claims is the only interesting part, is a speech by Hitler and it is missing from the surviving print. *Day of Freedom* is precisely what Riefenstahl admits it to be: a minor film made to satisfy the petty jealousies of German generals.

CHAPTER III

OLYMPIA

Many words have been used to describe Leni Riefenstahl's two-part film on the 1936 Berlin Olympics: a poem, a hymn, a paean, an ode to beauty. Whatever word or phrase is chosen, they all point to the same conclusion: that this monumental effort by Leni Riefenstahl stands as one of the greatest moments of beauty in the history of the cinema, a beauty of the modern art form that rivals the classical beauty of the ancients.

There is a popular myth that Riefenstahl's *Olympia* was the first Olympic film made. The first Olympic film was made, however, by her discoverer and mentor, Dr. Arnold Fanck, who in 1928 made a film of the St. Moritz International Winter Olympics entitled *Das Weisse Stadion* (The White Stadium). Although the film had the permission and the support of the International Olympics Committee, it was a low-key, low-budget affair, employing only two cameramen, the veteran Fanck cameramen Sepp Allgeier and Hans Schneeberger, along with two assistants, Albert Benitz and Richard Angst. The completed film was 2200 meters long, or slightly under the average feature length, and was divided into six different parts.

In his memoirs, Fanck admits that he wasn't very interested in making the film, since he regarded dramatic feature films, not documentaries, as his specialty. It is clear that his reasons for making the film were purely financial, and the commercial failure of the Ufa-backed film proves the trust a misplaced one. Fanck later mused that all that is necessary to make a documentary is film and to be present at the event, which conveniently freed his evenings for roulette-playing at an exclusive St. Moritz resort hotel. His attitude is quite a contrast to what Riefenstahl would demonstrate during the Berlin Olympic Games.

Fanck further stated that although his cameramen shot over 30,000 meters of film, Ufa gave him only 17 days to edit the film. His response was panic, and he turned to Walter Ruttmann for help. The film was quickly put together, but not even Ruttmann's contribution could rescue it from mediocrity. Although the photography has been described as interesting, the film was a bore and almost instantly forgotten.

In 1932, an attempt was made to make a film of the Olympic Games then being held in Los Angeles. Although a considerable amount of footage was shot, no film emerged. Covering the entire International Olympic Games was an effort still to be successfully undertaken. Leni Riefenstahl's film was to be the first, and from a commercial standpoint, one of the few successful filmings of the International Olympic Games.

The idea to film the 1936 Berlin Games did not originate with Leni Riefenstahl. The idea first occurred to a friend of Riefenstahl's, Professor Carl Diehm of Berlin, who had seen *Triumph of the Will* and was impressed with how it had handled such a massive event. Coincidentally, Professor Diehm happened to observe Riefenstahl training one day at the Berlin Stadium. She had always been interested in gymnastics, and at that time she was putting herself through rigorous physical exercises in an attempt to win athletic certification. Seeing Riefenstahl training at the site of the future Olympic Games, and with *Triumph of the Will* still fresh in his memory, Diehm had the notion that Riefenstahl should expand on her experience and film the Olympic Games. He proposed the idea to Riefenstahl and then brought it to another of his personal friends, Herr Maier, who happened to be the chairman of the International Olympics Committee. The proposal met with interest from both parties, and the first steps towards the making of *Olympia* were taken.

Unlike her reluctance to film *Penthesilea* in the early 1930's, Riefenstahl felt confident that she could make the Olympics film. Further, she felt that only she had the qualifications to seriously attempt the project. Her experience in making *Triumph of the Will* had given her unique training that no one else had been afforded: how to film a massive event occurring in many different locations over a considerable period of time, with thousands of participants and spectators. Not only was she convinced that she could film the games in a suitable documentary manner, but her confidence in her own artistic abilities assured her that she would be able to capture the spirit as well as the physical reality of the games. Once more her challenge was to make a film that transcended newsreel reportage, and to provide viewers with a genuine insight into the true beauties and hardships of the international competition.

The approval of the international and the German Olympic committees was secured, and it was only a matter of finding adequate commercial backing to make the project possible. To the German film producers of the day, it appeared to be a risky proposition. Riefenstahl's plans were far more elaborate than Fanck's crude attempt in 1928. But providing such large financing for an unproven documentary, even after the success of *Triumph of the Will,* proved to be more of a gamble than Ufa was willing to undertake. Riefenstahl then turned to Ufa's major competitor, TOBIS, and received the backing she needed. The conventional wisdom of the industry was that TOBIS was taking a foolhardy risk.

Filming 136 different competitions was not a challenge to be taken lightly. Riefenstahl assembled a camera crew of 48 individuals, including six major cameramen and sixteen assistants. They trained for the Olympic Games by filming German sports events, giving them a feel for the action that was awaiting them. According to the official book about the film, *Leni Riefenstahl's Olympia-Film,* written by Ernst Jäger[1], the Haus Ruhwald, a stately Berlin villa, was placed at the disposal of the film crew and 120 beds were set up throughout the halls and rooms of the building. Forty automobiles were made available for the staff.

One of the most noteworthy aspects of the making of *Olympia* is the camera crew. Although Riefenstahl complains that she was unable to get the top cameramen she wanted because they were under contract elsewhere, there are some notable names in the list. Perhaps the best known is Willy Hameister, who was the cameraman for the 1919 expressionist classic *The Cabinet of Dr. Caligari*. Other names are familiar from the Fanck films, such as Kurt Neubert and Hans Gottschalk, who had been cameramen for Fanck, and Hans Ertl, Guzzi Lantschner, and Heinz von Jaworsky, who had either acted in Fanck's films or served as mountaineering assistants. The ranks of the cameramen also included a number of inexperienced operators, and for some (such as Hans Ertl and Guzzi Lantschner) it was their first major assignment. Although they were constantly under her watch, Riefenstahl's opinion is that the younger, inexperienced cameramen were often better than the old veterans. Their lack of experience often made them more inventive and more capable of filming under difficult conditions than the older and more tradition-bound experts. According to Riefenstahl's estimates, the average age of the cameramen was 25. Riefenstahl was 34.

The six major cameramen were the only ones allowed to film in the stadium itself. Since minute organization was necessary under such circumstances, each of the six was given a special assignment and area of responsibility. Hans Ertl was in charge of the underwater photography and the running events; Walter Frentz was given the sailing regatta, the marathon race (particularly the hand camera shots), and the shots to be filmed from an anchored balloon; Guzzi Lantschner, the training, riding, gymnastics, swimming, and rowing events; Kurt Neubert was placed in charge of the

slow-motion photography; Hans Scheib handled the telephoto shots; and Willy Zielke was to film the prologue.

Beyond the major cameramen, each of whom had assigned
assistants, there were ten cameramen sent out into the crowds
to film unobserved reaction shots.

Riefenstahl did not attempt to write a shooting script
before the filming began. She knew that such a film could
only be constructed later, in the editing rooms. But she did
make several decisions about the film's general construction
before starting the project. First, she concluded that the film
had to have two parts, instead of being one unified entity.
Since she regarded the track and field events to be the heart
of the Olympic Games, she envisioned them as constituting
the first part. After its completion, it was given the title *Fest
der Völker* (Festival of the People). The decathlon, which she
regarded, along with the marathon and the hundred-meter
dash as one of the most important events of the games, was to
form the core of the second part, to be entitled *Fest der
Schönheit* (Festival of Beauty).

For Riefenstahl, there was only one possible way to begin
the film, and that was with a prologue that would bring the
audience back into the days of ancient Greece and the origins
of the Olympic Games. Foregoing words and propelling the
film along only with the quiet strains of Herbert Windt's
score, Riefenstahl establishes yet another of her stylized
dreams by tracking the camera slowly through temple ruins
and visually caressing classical statues strewn along the way.
The camera finally settles on the famous statue of the discus
thrower. Suddenly, the statue begins to come to life. In a slow
dissolve, the statue becomes a real-life figure. Riefenstahl had
observed that Huber, the German decathlon champion, had
the same physique as the figure in the Myron statue, and she
conceived the idea of dissolving from the statue to the live
figure bent in the same pose. The atmosphere in this scene
and throughout the prologue sequence is striking. It has a soft
gray, dreamlike quality, with dark tones establishing its

setting in the past. In the quality of its tones, it is one of the most captivating examples of Riefenstahl's stylization and her ability to translate private dreams to the reality of the screen.

From the discus thrower, the camera moves on to show other classical sports in the same dreamlike manner: the javelin throw and then the shot put. A close-up shot shows the shot-put thrower tossing the ball from hand to hand in rhythmic, dance-like motions. This shot becomes another dissolve, as the masculine arms of the shot-put thrower become the feminine arms of dancers. An erotic and very expressionistic dance is performed by several nude women, including Riefenstahl herself (although her anonymity is protected by the camera angle).[2] The dance was conceived by Riefenstahl, and was shot in the sand dunes of a Baltic beach.

Riefenstahl intended that the dancers represent the ancient Greek temple dancers, the keepers of the sacred flame. She establishes this symbolism by dissolving from the dancer's form into a flame, which then becomes the flame of the Olympic Games torch.

The 1936 Olympic Games were the first modern Olympics in which the torch was carried from Olympia in Greece to the site of the games. It was a dramatic idea, and one that Riefenstahl wanted to capture in her film. But when she arrived on the scene, she found the official ceremony quite disappointing. Gimmicks such as the use of parabolic mirrors to light the torch simply did not fit into her conception of the prologue, so she staged her own lighting ceremony in the ancient stadium of Delphi, using a young man whose physique fit her notions of classical beauty. The atmospheric quality of her prologue was not only preserved but enhanced through this bit of theatrical staging. The discus thrower coming to life, the sensuous nude dancers, and the young Greek standing at the Olympic fire establish at the very beginning of the film the fascination with the beauty of the human body that concerns Riefenstahl throughout *Olympia*. It is a very personal vision, but it is also a reflection of the standards of beauty and perfection that have prevailed throughout the history of art. Riefenstahl expresses these standards in a modern medium, but the ideas are old. That is the message of the prologue.

Once the torch is lit, the film follows the flame as it is carried from Greece to Germany, first by using footage of the runners, and then following their progress on a map of Europe. The physical journey of the flame becomes a travel in time. By the time the Olympic Stadium is seen from the air and the roar of the crowds and the pealing of the Olympic bell are heard, the audience has been transported from ancient Greece to the contemporary reality of 1936, and the documentary story of the Berlin 1936 Olympic Games begins.

When making a documentary that cannot be controlled or rehearsed, the director always runs the risk that the film will be less a director's than a cameraman's creation. This danger is increased by the physical impossibility of the director's being at simultaneously held events. For Riefenstahl, however, an overpowering desire to control all aspects of the film's creation, buttressed by formidable technical skills, minimized the threat of the film being anyone's but her own. She personally surveyed the location of each event and studied its nature. Armed with the information from these observations, she personally chose the camera placement and angles and issued the necessary instructions to the cameramen. Her control extended to choosing the lenses, type of film, and camera speed. As Heinz Jaworsky, one of her cameramen, later observed: "She told every cameraman what to do in precise detail, what lens to use, what filter to use, what sequence to shoot."[3] In her relations with her cameramen, Riefenstahl always had the final word. And to make sure of that, production meetings of all the cameramen, production staff, and the director were held each night to review what had been done during the day and what would be happening the next day. Any weary member caught napping during the late-night sessions was admonished by Riefenstahl with, "In three weeks you can sleep."

An example of Riefenstahl's elaborate preparations is her selection of what kind of film to use. She experimented with every major film on the market, and after extensive tests, discovered that each had a characteristic quality that the others didn't have. Agfa, she discovered, was best for buildings, sculpture, and stonework; Kodak was best with people and faces; and the newly marketed Perutz film was best with outdoor shots and nature scenes. Rather than make any sacrifice to quality, Riefenstahl decided to use all three in *Olympia*. The production manager in charge of film (over 80,000 feet of film was shot per day) merely issued the film each day to the cameramen according to what they would be shooting. As a further protection, Riefenstahl had a special processing lab installed to process the film immediately each day. Three cutters were assigned to the lab to view the film as soon as it was processed and to make a full report on the quality of the filming at each evening's production meeting. With these precautions, Riefenstahl was able to monitor daily the progress of the film.

Camera placement was always of key importance for the film, for the inventive use of angles could easily mean the difference between a boring and a fascinating film. Since each event had its own distinctive nature, there was no universal rule that could be formulated and uniformly applied. Each situation required serious consideration before the camera could be set up. Riefenstahl soon discovered, however, that the event often provided a key for her to follow. She noted:

> Each time, it was necessary that I think about things in order to find the reason for the camera's position in relation to this or that event. . . . Little by little, I discovered that the constraints imposed at times by the event could often serve me as a guide. The whole thing lay in knowing when and how to respect or violate these constraints. Thus, there were some perspectives that had to be respected.[4]

Once she had decided on the desired placement and angle, the next difficulty was how to obtain it. Often, the camera placement that she decided was best for the event was also physically the most difficult. It was her success in obtaining these placements that made *Olympia* a truly innovative film, establishing precedents for filmed sports coverage that continue to the present day, as well as inventing new devices to facilitate the filming. The examples abound as each obstacle is confronted and overcome. To capture close-ups of swimmers in the Olympic pool, and then to move away from the close-up at a time when zoom lenses were not yet available, a special rubber boat was used with the camera attached to a frame at the edge of the boat. The boat was then pushed in the pool with poles rather than using oars, which would have rocked the boat and caused an unsteady picture. To film runners on a track, a camera was designed to run on a catapult that was parallel to the track. The catapult had an adjustable speed so that the camera was always a few steps ahead of the runner. For the rowing races, a rail platform was built across the water so that the camera dollies could follow the rowers. For other ground events, pushed wheel dollies were used to provide zoom effects. To obtain her "trade-mark" low-angle shots, pits were dug along the side of tracks, allowing for a close-up as well as a low-angle view of the runners. To avoid disturbing the competitors while keeping such close proximity, special soundproofing compartments were designed for the cameras so that their operation could not be heard by those close at hand. Such "barneys" and "blimps" are now standard film equipment.

In order to obtain close-ups when proximity was not permissible, telescopic lenses were employed. For creative angles during the swimming and diving competition, a traveling crane capable of going over the pool was utilized. And for panorama shots of the main stadium, Riefenstahl had collapsible steel towers designed that could be placed in the middle of the stadium and moved when needed.

Some of Riefenstahl's plans were less successful. She had hoped to film the sculling races from a balloon (which at that time were as common as helicopters are today, and used for much the same purposes), but the International Olympics Committee refused permission for the excursion. Riefenstahl's angry and reportedly tearful protestations were to no avail. Another plan to use a small balloon to hover over the stadium while a remote-controlled camera strapped to it took overhead shots produced footage too blurry to use. In another experiment, a miniaturized camera (the Kinamo) that carried only 16½ feet of 35mm film was strapped to the chests of the marathon runners during their training. The camera was pointed at their feet, and was intended to film the runner's view of his legs traveling over the ground. The first results were completely unusable, so experiments were made with different film speeds and, finally, a slightly larger camera capable of holding 100 feet instead of 16½. With over 1000 feet of film exposed, only a few small pieces were eventually good enough to use, although they did obtain the desired effect.

Of all the inventions and techniques pioneered by Riefenstahl in *Olympia,* certainly the most memorable is the underwater photography of Hans Ertl during the famous diving sequence. Ertl designed a special watertight housing for his Sinclair camera that would enable him to film the diver as he left the board, and then follow the diver under water and continue filming in one continuous take. To do this, Ertl had to adjust for distance during the dive, change the exposure setting as soon as the diver went under water, and then reverse the process when following the diver back to the surface. A small elevator apparatus mounted to the side of the pool, on which Ertl sat, gave him the smooth continuous motion needed. It was a new technique for its time and required considerable practice to gain the rapid dexterity required for all the manual operations. But it provides some of the most stunning photography in the film.

When Riefenstahl chose to restage the torchlighting scene in her stylized manner for the prologue, it had no effect on the documentary aspects of the film since the prologue is an entity separate from the recording of the games in the rest of the film. But conditions necessitated other restagings during the film as well. Some were done to enhance the film artistically, but most were done simply because conditions did not permit otherwise. Two major events are totally restaged in the film. The first is the pole vault finals, where the American champion Glenn Morris was a major contender. The finals were held at night, and the Olympics Committee would not allow Riefenstahl to erect the strong lights needed to film the scene because of fear that they would distract the competing athletes. Since she did not have the alternative of the extremely light-sensitive film that is available today, it was a question of either restaging the event later under proper conditions or excluding this important part of the Olympics from the film altogether. So the following evening, Riefenstahl assembled (with the help of Glenn Morris) the two Japanese and three American finalists and returned to the stadium to restage the event. There were no major events in the stadium at the time, so there was no difficulty in setting up the powerful lights. Riefenstahl recalls that after an initial shyness, the competitive spirit crept back into the athletes until they were performing with the same vigor that they had exhibited the night before. The same difficulty occurred later with the 1500-meter run in the decathlon competitions, and the same solution was employed.

Such liberties would be inexcusable in historical newsreel footage. But it was not Riefenstahl's intention to capture on film the history-making record heights in pole vaulting or the record-setting running times. Her camera is concerned with the participants more than with the event, and in recording their emotions as they strain at the starting block or when the deciding jump arrives. It is both an aesthetic study of the performance of the human body and a psychological study of the emotions of the participants. With this in mind, it doesn't matter that the event seen in the film is not the historic event. What is seen has the same participants, the same location, and the same challenge, with all three repeating history as well as serving the needs of Riefenstahl's art.

Riefenstahl did feel obliged to film each major award ceremony as a final tribute to the victorious athletes, but she realized that these ceremonies would quickly become repetitious and boring if they were not varied somehow. She attempted to film each in a different manner; some were in close-up, others long shots, and with varied angles. Also, she restaged two or three of the ceremonies so that she would be free to experiment with the composition.

No matter how important the photography was for *Olympia*, it is still through the editing that the film gains its fame. Riefenstahl is a consistent artist; she experiments, but always within the framework of her established principles. She followed in *Olympia* the same editing concepts that she had established for *Triumph of the Will*. The concept of peaks and valleys developed for *Triumph of the Will* is even more noticeable in *Olympia*. Besides seeking high and low levels of emotion, she extended the concept to the other aspects of the film: the music, tone, and content as well as the form. If there was an event of great dramatic tension, such as the rowing competition, she tried to break the level of tension by following the event immediately with one of a light and humorous nature—in this instance, the horseback-riding scene where the mounted horses falling into the water pits provide humorous relief from the tension of the previous scene.

In the same manner, Riefenstahl varied the aural texture of the film, applying the same montage principles to sound mixing that she did to film editing. She tried to balance noise and music throughout the film. For some events, it was impossible to add a music background. A 100-meter dash would have its dramatic tension ruined by music; here the tension is much better buttressed by roars of the crowd than musical chords. On the other hand, an event such as the hurdles, which was so dance-like and graceful in nature, cried out for a musical accompaniment.

A good example of this sound-mixing concept is the pole vault competition. This event was divided into two parts: the preliminaries, which occurred during the day, and the finals, held at night. The dead-heat finals in the evening, which she later restaged, were sufficient to depict the pole vault competition. So for the filming of the first part, she concentrated on capturing the grace of the athletes' movements, rendering them through editing into a ballet that was fully orchestrated with music.

At the end of the games, Riefenstahl found that covering the games was a minor task compared to the challenge that now confronted her: the editing of 400,000 meters (approximately 1.3 million feet) of film into a coherent whole. Her first step was to simply run through all the footage to evaluate the material she had to work with. That took ten weeks of steady viewing, often more than ten hours per day. After she had viewed the footage, she began to organize the next steps with the personal efficiency that is one of her trademarks. In her personal and business life, Riefenstahl has a penchant for order and organization that is almost manic. But that is a talent that would enable her to meet a challenge the mere contemplation of which would overwhelm most people.

Five large editing rooms were used for *Olympia*. Four were for positive footage and the fifth for the original negative. In each room, she had large glass partitions constructed on which she could hang strips of film down to the floor level for quick viewing. The partitions were also a help in examining the footage for tonal quality. Furthermore, all footage was neatly cataloged according to a system designed by Riefenstahl. A number system was used for each event, such as 10 for the 100-meter dash. Each segment within the event, such as the qualifiers, the placement, and the deciding event, was also assigned its own number, such as 10-1, 10-2. Once all the film was cataloged, Riefenstahl was able to find the exact piece of footage that she wanted within a matter of seconds.[5] With 400,000 meters of film to work with, the absence of such a system could only mean chaos.

Riefenstahl spent eighteen months editing *Olympia*. Her only assistants were those who helped in the physical chores of editing, such as splicing and filing the footage. The actual editing she reserved to herself, refusing to surrender the artistic control she values so highly. During those eighteen months, she often worked around the clock, becoming so consumed with her work that she would forego meals and sleep. Her friends and relatives began to worry for her sanity as she lost herself completely in the editing rooms. All personal life was canceled until the film was completed.

Fanatic devotion to her work is one of Riefenstahl's primary traits. A lesser artist would have been content to spend only a fraction of that time editing the film. But the artistic perfection that Riefenstahl created in *Olympia* would have been lost. Her own words reveal why:

> I could have edited the film in half the time, if I hadn't been so thorough, but I had to try everything, every kind of cross-cutting experiment. Once I had edited a section or a sequence, for instance the marathon, it ought to have been finished and OK. But then I started wondering whether it couldn't be done still better. So I made perhaps 100, 200 or more different trial editings. It was my time and it didn't earn me any money, but it was a challenge. I tried for the best possible result I felt I could get out of it, irrespective of time, health, or anything else, least of all money.[6]

By the time the editing was complete, the shooting ratio was a staggering sixty to one. The editing plays its most important role in the two best-known sequences of the film: the marathon race and the diving competition.

When Riefenstahl first considered the marathon race, she couldn't imagine how she would ever render the event cinematically and still keep the audience interested. A marathon race is certainly not a spectator sport. It's very length makes it impossible for the audience to observe or even sympathize with it in total, and the only concentrated moment of tension is at the very end. But merely to film the start and finish would be unfair to what Riefenstahl knew was the most grueling and demanding event of the games. It was in the marathon race that the qualities of endurance and of mind over body reached their greatest heights, and she resolved to set these qualities to film. But how?

The answer came when Riefenstahl decided to concentrate on the mental strain exerted on each runner as his physical exhaustion grew. She wanted to put the audience into the mind and body of the participants, to show what it was like to run for such a long distance, and to make the audience feel the strength dwindling from the body. At this point the film departs from the documentary mode again and becomes more like the prologue. The small Kinamo camera was used to film the passing ground as it appeared to the runner. Then subjective tracking shots of the passing scenery were filmed, following the viewpoint of the runner as he ran down the track and looked at the people watching him. Edited-in nature shots of trees and gently moving grass added a poetic quality to the atmosphere of the sequence.

Again, the decision was made to stylize reality. The sequence was to become a filmic ode to "the loneliness of the long-distance runner." Distorted shadows, almost expressionistic in appearance, were inserted, showing the runner's form moving along the empty stretches of road. The audience is made to see and feel movement. The pounding legs of the runner shown by the Kinamo camera give a sensation of the energy being expended. Sound is also brought into play. Nearing the end of the race and on the last burst of energy, the runners hear the noises of the stadium crowd, signaling the approaching finish line. The crowd noises spur them on to another burst of energy. A fanfare of trumpets invokes a sense of the medieval as well as contemporary reality. A runner's legs are shown in slow motion to stress further the burden the runner is suffering. The sequence ends with the crowd noises growing louder as the image dissolves into the Olympic Stadium.

The composition of the diving sequence presents a contrast to the staged stylization of the marathon race. In this sequence, Riefenstahl uses the reality of the event, and nothing else, to create on the editing table what can best be described as a "symphony of movement." Like the marathon race, the diving competition by its very nature could have been one of the most uninteresting in the film. Each dive, no matter how technically perfect in execution, tends to look like the previous one after three or four have been shown. Again, Riefenstahl decided against merely recording the event. Fascinated by the movements of the divers, she made their movements the cornerstone of her editing. Each cut becomes a matchcut, based on the movements of the dive before and after it. The camera angles add to the heroic nature of the shots, providing the familiar background of billowy clouds.

The most striking aspect of the editing in the diving sequence is its complete suspension of the physical realities of motion, space, and time. The divers appear in the sky as if from nowhere and perform the most beautiful movements while suspended in space, apparently defying all laws of gravity. Depicted in slow motion, their movements become surreal. One after another, bodies fly through the air in complete defiance of all laws of natural science. It is pure cinematic invention, a creation of beauty that although constructed from fragments of physical reality has nothing to do with what was actually seen in the Olympic pools that day.

The perfectionism that Riefenstahl practiced in the editing rooms did not stop there; it continued in the sound studios and even in the processing labs. When she arrived at the mixing studios of TOBIS, Riefenstahl had with her up to sixteen different sound tracks per shot: speakers, music, crowd noises, shouting groups and more, often several variations of each. The sound engineers insisted that it was impossible to use all of them, but after Riefenstahl persisted they set out to do the impossible. Just as when the cameraman Schneeberger once argued with Riefenstahl's impossible notion of using a certain filter during *The Blue Light,* Riefenstahl's intuition proved better than the specialist's knowledge. New noise-filtering systems were devised to give Riefenstahl exactly what she wanted. She often found that to obtain the sound effect that she wanted, she had to redo her editing: "I had to recut the sound as well as the picture, to lengthen one shot to take in a sound effect completely, or shorten another to cut out clashes. And to modify the sound or the image, every one of the eight to sixteen sound tracks needed altering."[7]

When the editing and mixing were finally completed, Riefenstahl accompanied the negative to the printing lab to oversee personally the print exposure of the first six release prints. Riefenstahl knew that her carefully planned and achieved experiments in tonal qualities, using the three different film types and carefully selected filters, could be easily sabotaged by sloppy printing of the release prints. If a shot were printed too light or dark, it would lose its impact and its artistic importance would be lost. While she was monitoring the first six prints, she trained an assistant to be aware of exactly what she wanted so he could take charge of printing the rest before they were sent to theaters around Germany and the world. Initially, some 450 release prints were made.

Rarely in the history of cinema prior to *Olympia* had a filmmaker extended such control over all aspects of the film's creation. It is certainly the rule for most commercial film undertakings to have production assistants in charge of specialized features of the film's production, to have a professional editor edit the film, a studio mixer handle the mixing, and to leave the printing of the release prints to professionals in the lab. But Riefenstahl took personal charge of each of these aspects. She selected the film, the lenses, the filters, the camera placements, and gave the minutest instructions to each cameraman. She did the editing and supervised the sound mixing and printing. It was not a question of interfering in areas in which she had no knowledge. Several of her cameramen had learned their trade from Riefenstahl, and all realized that she was as competent as any of them to run the camera. She had learned editing the hard way but the only way, first through observing Fanck edit his films, and then through trial and error on her own in *The Blue Light* and *Triumph of the Will*. She learned sound mixing and printing the same way and had once encamped in a processing laboratory until she had learned every detail, down to the correct developer temperature. If she argued with the professionals, she knew what she was talking about.

The critical acclaim for *Olympia* began with the film's premiere on April 20, 1938, in Berlin. It won the Grand Prize at that year's International Film Festival in Venice, where it was cited as "the world's best film of 1938." Prizes were also awarded by the Greek and Swedish governments. Most surprising of all was a letter of praise for the film sent by Stalin to the Russian ambassador in Berlin, along with instructions to invite Riefenstahl to visit Moscow.[8]

The strange exception to the disseminators of critical praise for *Olympia* was the United States. Anti-Nazi sentiment frightened potential distributors away from the film, and it was never shown commercially there. When Riefenstahl made her first visit to the United States in 1938, a boycott was organized against her. One of the leaders of the boycott was Budd Schulberg, who at the end of the war wrote an inflammatory article for *The Saturday Evening Post* entitled "Leni Riefenstahl—Nazi Pinup Girl" which repeated the same unsubstantiated charges against Riefenstahl that prompted the boycott.[9]

Despite the charges that *Olympia* was a propaganda film for the Nazis (leveled by people who, because of their own boycott, had never seen the film), a few critics were brave enough to give Riefenstahl the benefit of the doubt and view the film. Among them was Walt Disney, whose own film *Snow White and the Seven Dwarfs* had also been a serious contender for best film at the Venice Festival. Disney was one of the few Hollywood notables to receive Riefenstahl openly. And those who saw the film at a few private screenings given by Riefenstahl in Hollywood were surprised by it. One was a United Press correspondent named Henry McLemore who covered the Berlin Olympics. Here is his report:

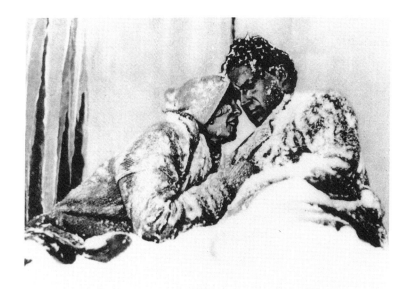

Above: Maria (Leni Riefenstahl) and her husband Heinz (Gustav Diessl) trapped and freezing on a mountain ledge in Dr. Fanck's film *The White Hell of Piz Palu*. **Below:** Fanck filmed *S.O.S. Iceberg* on location in Greenland. Starring Leni Riefenstahl, it featured the aerial exploits of the famous World War I flying ace Ernst Udet.

Above: A small village with an idyllic mountain waterfall provides the setting for the romantic, legendary story of *The Blue Light*. **Below:** A shot from *The Blue Light* typical of Riefenstahl's visual style: Junta (played by Riefenstahl) silhouetted against a backdrop of drifting clouds.

Above and below: Riefenstahl's refusal to film more difficult scenes in the safety of a studio led to some difficult shots in the Dolomites.

Above: Instead of professional actors, Riefenstahl used villagers from the small village of Sarentino for *The Blue Light*. **Below:** A break during the filming of *The Blue Light*. Riefenstahl is seated in the front, while fellow scriptwriter Béla Bálazs leans on the carriage door.

An elevator on the flagpole behind the rostrum allowed high-angle shots of Hitler's address to the S.A. Construction of the elevator was one of rally architect Albert Speer's few concessions on the filming of the Nuremberg Party Rally for *Triumph of the Will.*

Above and below: Myron's famous statue of the discus thrower comes to life in the prologue of *Olympia*.

Above: Riefenstahl made an anonymous appearance as a nude dancer in the *Olympia* prologue. **Below:** Reenacting the Olympic torchlighting ceremony of ancient Greece.

Above: A camera crew uses the Olympic diving board to obtain overhead shots of the swimming competition. **Below:** A striking feature of *Triumph of the Will* and *Olympia:* composition within the frame.

Above: Using a special emulsion, Riefenstahl filmed outdoor settings in *Tiefland* with a painting-like quality. **Below:** Pedro strangles a wolf stalking his flock in the opening sequence of *Tiefland*.

Above: Peasant crops wither in the drought when water is diverted for the Marquis's herd of prize cattle in *Tiefland*. **Below:** In her role as Marta in *Tiefland*, Riefenstahl dances again.

Above: Marta (Leni Riefenstahl) and her guitarist friend arrive at the castle of the Marquis Sebastian. **Below:** The old shepherd arrives in the mountains to speak with Pedro.

Above: Marta, now a permanent resident at the castle, rides off with the Marquis to inspect his cattle. **Below:** As in *The Blue Light,* the peasants in *Tiefland* were carefully selected to show the weathered look of people living close to nature.

Above: Marta swoons after being struck by the Marquis. **Below:** Pedro finds Marta's exhausted body in the mountains after she flees from the Marquis.

Above: The old shepherd awaits Pedro's return from the valley. **Below:** Leaving the greed of the lowlands behind, Marta and Pedro return arm-in-arm to the purity of the mountains in the final scene of *Tiefland*.

Riefenstahl in Africa, 1965.

Filming the Nuba, 1974.

Last night I saw the finest motion picture that I have
ever seen, and you mustn't dismiss my opinion lightly,
because as a man who dates back to John Bunny, Flora
Finch, "Broken Blossoms" and "Birth of a Nation," I am
qualified to speak as a fairly competent critic.

. . . Few persons in this country ever have seen the
film. I have heard that it will never be extensively shown
because of the anti-Nazi boycott and the belief that it
consists of German propaganda. The show that I saw was
in the nature of a secret one—a sort of sneak preview, in
which those invited were asked not to mention the time
nor the place in which they saw it.

I am not in favor of any such handling of the film. It is
not propaganda, but a magnificent filming of the
greatest athletes in the history of the world. It could
have been taken anywhere—England, France, Greece,
or Switzerland. If it is not shown to the youth of this
country, the youth of this country will be the loser.
From start to finish—and it runs almost four hours—its
only message is the joy and the glory that comes from
the development of a superb body. . . . [10]

McLemore's enthusiasm was shared in an unsigned editorial appearing in the *Los Angeles Times:*

While it is not to be released in America, according to
present plans, because of anti-Nazi controversies, the
motion picture record of the XI Olympiad, produced by
Leni Riefenstahl, a visitor here, was given a private
showing this week in Los Angeles, and revealed itself as
far more than simply a chronicle of world-renowned
competition, but a triumph for the camera and an epic
poem of the screen.

It is regrettable that political issues should intrude to
prevent the general distribution of the feature in
America, because contrary to rumor, it is in no way a
propaganda production but simply a superfine camera
analysis of great athletic events accomplished with art
and imagination which are truly international in scope.

The picture idealizes the spirit of the Olympiad, going
back to Athens of old for its prologue, and ending
practically in the stratosphere with its visioning of
swimmers and divers performing their grace-beatified

feats seemingly far above the terrestrial sphere, followed by a pageant of light effects of unrivaled character.

. . . As a record of the finest contests in the athletic
field, it is surpassingly comprehensive, and endlessly
fascinating, and as propaganda for any one country or
any one people its effect is definitely nil.[11]

Even though several important film critics have made the
accusation that *Olympia* is Nazi propaganda, it is difficult to
understand their conclusions in light of the film itself.
References are made to the presence of Hitler in the film,
such as Susan Sontag's observation of the games as being "all
under the gaze of the benign Super-Spectator, Hitler, whose
presence in the stadium consecrates this effort."[12] Perhaps
some people, the previous critic included, are so awed by the
physical presence of Hitler that he assumes mystical propor-
tions, but that is not the cumulative effect of the few times
Hitler is actually shown in the film. The only major section
that does feature Hitler is his official opening of the games,
filmed in a straightforward documentary manner. Riefenstahl
gives it the same treatment she would have if the games had
been held in Moscow and the opening done by Joseph Stalin.
There are no more shots of Hitler than would have been
devoted to the head of state of any host country, and some of
the shots, particularly those of Goering, show the Nazi
leaders in clowning and far-from-inspiring poses as their
emotions get the better of their self-control.

Equally important is the fact that the true hero of the film
is not Adolf Hitler but the black American athlete Jesse
Owens. It is Owens' presence that dominates the first part of
Olympia, and Riefenstahl gives his athletic triumphs the full
cinematic coverage they deserved rather than downplaying
them in the name of Nazi racial ideology. In fact, Propaganda
Chief Goebbels ordered Riefenstahl to delete the footage of
Owens, and when she refused, government sanctions were
temporarily placed on her film company.

Riefenstahl stresses the international nature of the Olympic competition. Her concern is with the athletes as individuals, and there is no touting of the Germans as members of a "master race" as would be expected if the film were Nazi propaganda. Although the Nazi flag was the dominant flag of *Triumph of the Will,* it is the International Olympic flag and not the German flag that dominates *Olympia.* As one critic has observed, *Olympia* can be seen as a complete reversal, if not a refutation, of what was shown in *Triumph of the Will.* At the end of *Triumph of the Will,* the Nazi standards representing the various regions of Germany are paraded into the Congress Hall, a visual symbolization of the unity of the German state; but in *Olympia,* the ending shows the national flags dissolving into the Olympic flag as the international spirit triumphs over national feelings.[13] Hardly an example of Nazi nationalism!

Other critics have observed that in stressing the competitiveness of the events and glorifying the superhuman feats of strength, the "triumph of the will" needed to win in the fierce Olympic competition, Riefenstahl reflects the spirit of fascism. This view seems more to question the nature of sports events in general and the Olympics in particular than it does Riefenstahl and her film. Equating competitiveness with fascism is surely a risky critical assumption.

A question often asked is why Riefenstahl didn't film the 1938 Winter Olympics as well. The answer is that these games were appropriated by Goebbels and his propaganda ministry, who wanted to make sure that at least one Nazi film was made of the Olympic Games. A considerable number of cameramen from Riefenstahl's Olympic crew were requisitioned by the ministry. The result, as with Fanck's 1928 attempt, was an uninteresting film with good photography. Overshadowed by *Olympia,* the film was quickly forgotten. The financial gamble taken by TOBIS proved to be a smart risk. Not only was a work of art created, but it was a financial success as well. By the end of October, 1938, six months after the film's premiere, the German receipts alone amounted to more than four million marks. Those who said that the games could never be filmed, along with those who thought that nobody would watch such a film, were now eating their words.

CHAPTER IV

TIEFLAND

No matter how much time and energy it cost Riefenstahl to make *Olympia,* the effort was nothing compared to what she would encounter in the making of *Tiefland,* her last complete feature film.

Despite the fact that Riefenstahl does not like the film and for years had removed it from circulation, keeping the only prints of it tucked away in her apartment, it is a beautiful and captivating film that expands on the work she started in *The Blue Light.* The film also contains explicitly stated social comment, perhaps Riefenstahl's personal reaction to her earlier political naiveté.

The inspiration for *Tiefland* came to Riefenstahl from a book she happened across one day, much like her chance hearing of the Junta legend in the Dolomites. It was a Spanish book, a collection of photographs by a famous Spanish photographer whose name Riefenstahl has now forgotten. She was captivated by the book and its images of Spain: pictures of Castille, the people, their native costumes, and of everyday life. These pictures gave Riefenstahl the desire to film this Spanish milieu in her own style.

Riefenstahl had also become acquainted with an opera entitled *Tiefland* ("Lowlands") by Eugen d'Albert. Although now rarely performed, the opera was a Berlin favorite in the 1920's.[1] She saw in the opera's Spanish locales the vehicle that she needed and transposed the opera into a film script. She secured the backing of Terra Film and at the end of April, 1934, was asked to go to Spain to begin the preparations for the film.

According to Riefenstahl, she was delighted at the chance to go to Spain at that moment since it provided her with a convenient excuse to leave the Nuremberg Party Rally film (*Triumph of the Will*) in Walter Ruttmann's hands. At first, the film's future seemed promising. One of Germany's most famous actors, Heinrich George, was engaged to play the lead male role of Sebastian, and veteran Fanck actor Sepp Rist was to play Pedro. Riefenstahl tried to hire the famous director G. W. Pabst to direct the film. Although Pabst was interested in the project, another opportunity arose for him and he declined. A young director, Alfred Abel, was then hired and Hans Schneeberger signed on as cameraman. A confident Riefenstahl then departed for Madrid.

At that point, the entire project began to unravel. Although Heinrich George had been hired for the lead, his schedule allowed him only twenty-one free days for the filming of *Tiefland* before his next commitment. Time deadlines became matters of the greatest urgency as Riefenstahl attempted to find the locations, arrange production details, and solve the myriad of problems that go into making a film. Her problems were complicated by Terra Film's failure to fulfill their obligations to the project. Promised money didn't arrive, deadlines weren't met, and Riefenstahl, waiting in a Madrid hotel with Schneeberger, Rist, and others, became desperate. Suddenly one day in early June, 1934, she collapsed in the lobby of her hotel, the victim of a nervous breakdown. She was forced to stay in a Madrid hospital during June and July. She returned to Germany in August of 1934, with the *Tiefland* project scuttled and orders for *Triumph of the Will* waiting for her.

During *Triumph of the Will, Olympia,* and even the unrealized *Penthesilea* film (see Chapter VI) *Tiefland* was laid aside but not forgotten. When *Penthesilea* collapsed and the war began, Riefenstahl looked for a project that would occupy her energies while still keeping her outside of the war effort, and particularly away from making propaganda films such as those being assigned to other major directors.

In 1939, with the outbreak of war, Riefenstahl organized a small film group composed of her veteran cameramen to make short films on the front. The purpose of the film unit was to keep her cameramen occupied in filmmaking and thus avoid fighting on the front. But on one of her initial visits to occupied Poland, she witnessed an atrocity that she would never forget. Some German soldiers had been shot by Polish guerillas, and in retribution, Polish hostages in a small village were forced to dig their own graves. When they were finished, they were executed in the graves. Riefenstahl was a horrified witness to the entire event. After the war, a German soldier who was present and who had taken pictures of the atrocity, including one picture of Riefenstahl in a crowd of onlookers with a petrified look and a scream frozen on her face, attempted to blackmail her with the photos. She rejected the blackmail attempt, and the photos were made public. But the effect of the photos was to prove Riefenstahl's claim of feeling revulsion during the occurrence. She made futile protestations to higher military authorities and then left Poland in disgust, vowing to do anything to keep away from the war. Although she had lost her interest in filming *Tiefland,* it beckoned her as a ready-made project to keep her away from war-related assignments. In 1940, Riefenstahl resumed work in Spain on *Tiefland,* six years after her first attempt. Like *The Blue Light,* the film was produced, directed, and scripted by Leni Riefenstahl.

Making *Tiefland* turned out to be a nightmare for Riefenstahl that would last throughout the war. Since the film contained no propaganda message important for the war effort, it had no priority and was constantly being preempted from studios and editing rooms for war-priority films. Later, because of wartime currency restrictions, Riefenstahl was no longer able to film in Spain and had to move the entire production to Mittenwald in Bavaria, where a model Spanish village was erected as a substitute for the real one. A studio that had been rented, paid for, and decorated was taken over for one of Goebbels' pet projects, Veit Harlan's film *Der*

Grosse König,[2] and *Tiefland* was left without a studio. The German archives are filled with correspondence related to Riefenstahl's difficulties in making the film. In late 1944 she was asked for a list of all manpower connected with her filmmaking (including those working on short films commissioned by the government through Leni Riefenstahl Film G.m.b.H.) and to justify their absence form the war effort. Later, when she tried to find sound editing tables for post-synchronization (over half of the film had been shot outside and had to be post-synchronized), she was unable to get them and was forced to make a special appeal for the construction of new tables to her old friend, Albert Speer, who as armaments minister was the virtual czar of the German economy. Speer turned down her plea.[3] Finally, a studio in Prague was made available and most of the studio scenes were completed by the end of 1944. But the editing had to wait until long after the war.

After her experience with *The Blue Light,* Riefenstahl had no desire to play the combined roles of director and star. She was not interested in assuming the role of Marta, the gypsy dancer, but wanted to direct the film and fulfill her original plans as she had first conceived them in 1934. She tried to engage the actress Hilde Krahl, but with no success. An attempt to sign Brigitte Horney met with the same result. Finally, failing to find a suitable actress for the role, Riefenstahl decided to take the role herself and set out looking for a director. But in this search she encountered even more difficulty and finally decided to abandon her reservations and assume both tasks.

The film's haunting music was scored by Herbert Windt, after a careful analysis of the original music from the opera (see Appendix B), and was performed for the film by the Vienna Philharmonic.

The opening shot of *Tiefland* establishes its debt to the mountain film genre: sharp, craggy mountain peaks are shot against a cloud backdrop, with day-for-night photography setting the scene in the nighttime. A flock of sheep is shown grazing in the mountains, with one shot dissolving into the next. Suddenly, there is a low-angle shot of a wolf on a ledge, framed against the clouds, looking at the sheep. Pedro, a shepherd, stirs in his sleep as the shadow of the wolf approaches the sheep. Pedro is alarmed by the baying of the sheep and arises to investigate. He is immediately attacked by the wolf, and a fierce struggle between the shepherd and the wolf ensues, convincingly filmed in close-up. After being bitten by the wolf and suffering a profusely bleeding wound, Pedro finally overpowers the wolf and strangles it. For this beautifully filmed and well-staged action sequence, four trained wolves were used and two were lost before the filming was completed.

With the death of the wolf, the sun rises over the mountains, and the idyllic mountain scene becomes filled with sunlight as the world awakens. The camera tilts down a beautiful cascading waterfall, much like the one seen in *The Blue Light.*

The action now changes from Pedro and his flock in the "Hochland" (highlands) to the peasants in the "Tiefland" (lowlands) below the mountains. Peasants are shown working at an irrigation ditch in a dusty plain. After a cut showing Pedro leading his flock down from the mountains, a herd of cattle is shown grazing in pasture in the lowlands. A nobleman and his helpers are mounted on horseback, watching over the herd. They are approached by a solemn-looking group of peasants all dressed in black.

The peasants bow to the nobleman, the Marquis Sebastian. "We need water for our fields," one of the peasants says. "It belongs to everyone. It comes from above, from the highlands."

Sebastian gives the peasants a stern look and with a shake of his head, replies, "No. I need the water for my cattle." The peasants bow silently, and the marquis rides off.

A lively banquet scene follows, attended by the Marquis Sebastian, the mayor, and other assorted dignitaries. It has been rumored that Sebastian is interested in the mayor's daughter, and as the other guests dance, Sebastian invites her to the balcony. The conventional romantic balcony scene does not develop, however, because the marquis is not so inclined. In a rude and demanding manner he proposes marriage to the mayor's daughter, frankly informing her that he needs her family's wealth to pay for his cattle. The marquis, despite his splendid castle and his power over the peasants, is in financial trouble.

Although she is attracted to Sebastian, the mayor's daughter is offended by his rude manner and leaves the room after informing him that she will consider his proposal. She storms across the dance floor, and the party is scandalously brought to a halt.

Meanwhile, Pedro has brought his flock down from the mountains and is now in the kitchen of the marquis's castle. He is eating supper at a table crowded with female servants of all ages. They are all attracted to this shy and innocent young man whose lack of experience seems to be offset by his good nature and sincerity. This comic scene has Pedro sitting alone at the head of a table while the women, sitting at the other end, taunt him. "Which one of us do you want?" one of them asks. "None of you," Pedro replies and gets up from the table. Before he leaves the room, he proudly shows the women the pelt of the wolf he strangled in the mountains.

Pedro leaves the women and walks through the village. He hears music and goes to the window of the local café. Peering in, he sees a crowd watching a gypsy woman dancing an excited flamenco dance. The gypsy is Marta, played by Riefenstahl. For the first time since *The Holy Mountain* (with the exception of the anonymous scene in the *Olympia* prologue), Riefenstahl gets to display her dancing talents on the screen.

As Pedro watches through the window, the carriage of the marquis drives up behind him. Sebastian hears the music and stops his carriage. When he approaches the café, Pedro walks up to him and hands him the wolf pelt. Sebastian asks Pedro if he killed the wolf, and when Pedro replies affirmatively,

Sebastian hands him a coin. "For every wolf you kill, you will receive another just like it," he informs Pedro. And with that, he throws the wolf pelt into the street and walks into the café.

Meanwhile, one member of the crowd has become so aroused by Marta's dancing that he can no longer control himself. He jumps up and pulls her into his arms, only to be instantly repulsed by the laughter of the crowd. The marquis enters the café and it suddenly becomes dead quiet. "You must dance for me," Sebastian tells Marta and leaves the café with her.

After this sequence, Pedro returns to his beloved mountains, only this time bringing a new love with him. As he walks towards the mountain peaks, he looks at the sky and sees Marta's face. Pedro's life will never be as uncomplicated as before.

Sebastian arrives at his castle with Marta and her companion, a disreputable-looking guitar player who is sent off to eat with the servants while Marta dines with the marquis. Seated at the supper table, the marquis asks Marta where she learned to dance. "I never learned," she replies, indicating her natural talent.

Accompanied on the guitar by the marquis, Marta begins to dance. But her dancing has the same effect on the marquis that it had on the drunken peasant in the café, and Sebastian is quickly aroused. He takes her into his arms, kisses her, and then carries her off in his arms. The scene ends with their retreating shadow on the floor.

The next morning, the guitar player is ordered out of the castle by the marquis, who had learned during the night that the guitarist had often beaten Marta.

An old shepherd is seen climbing the mountains, approaching Pedro who is sitting contemplatively near the summit. The old shepherd sits next to Pedro and begins talking. "I like it here in the mountains. I feel freer." And then turning to Pedro, he adds, "You've changed, Pedro. Something is different."

"I don't want to be alone anymore," Pedro says. He has

always been content living alone in the mountains but he now wants a wife.

"Have you got someone special in mind?" the old shepherd inquires. Staring dreamily into space, Pedro nods his head.

Down in the lowlands, the drought has worsened and the villagers line up at the town well for buckets of water. A village elder is pouring one bucket for each woman, and no more. An old woman asks for a second bucket, but is refused; there simply isn't enough water for two buckets each. The village is running dry and the peasants' fields are withering, but there is enough water for Sebastian's cattle.

Marta has now become a permanent resident of Sebastian's castle. Dressed in a fancy Castilian dress that Sebastian has given her, she rides with him to the range to inspect the cattle. As they ride through a crowd of villagers, they are met with looks of hate. Close-up shots of rugged peasant faces are reminiscent of similar shots of alpine villagers in *The Blue Light.* Sebastian is cursed by one of the older women. He raises his arm to strike her but is restrained by Marta. Angered, Sebastian kicks his horse and rides off.

By now Marta has started to realize what is happening in the village and the troubles being caused by Sebastian's greed. As the sole recipient of Sebastian's less than bountiful generosity, she has conscience pangs and sympathizes with the villagers. She visits the wife of the village miller to offer her help. When she asks "What can I do to help you?" she is told, "Ask him to speak with the peasants, to reason with them." With these words, Marta leaves.

A delegation of peasants outside Sebastian's castle is waiting for a chance to speak with him. They have been waiting for hours, but the marquis has refused to see them. Instead, he visits Marta in her room. He asks if he can do anything for her, and she has but one request. "Speak with the peasants. They have been waiting for hours." she pleads. Sebastian is so deeply in love with Marta that he cannot refuse her request.

Sebastian goes outside to meet with the peasants. They ask

him once again for water, pleading that their crops will burn without the water, and without their crops they will be unable to pay the marquis their feudal rent. "If that happens, you will be evicted," the marquis warns, and walks off. The peasants' faces reveal increasing hatred and there is an uneasy and no longer submissive air about them.

Marta, realizing the plight of the peasants, makes a desperate attempt to help them. Taking a priceless necklace given to her by Sebastian, she steals away to the village to talk again with the miller's wife. Marta gives her the necklace, with the instructions that it should be sold and the proceeds used to pay the rent to Sebastian.

When the miller returns in the evening with a hopeless look on his face, he is informed by his wife, "Today is our lucky day—we can pay the rent." She hands her husband the necklace and explains what has happened. Enraged, the husband shouts, "We don't want charity, we want our rights," and orders her to return the necklace. In the next scene, soldiers arrive at the mill and evict the miller and his family. They stand outside the mill, their few worldly possessions tied to a small cart.

Times are hard in the village, but the marquis is having his difficulties as well. Like the villagers, he has debts he cannot pay. And furthermore, his butler, who acts as his advisor, is a treacherous sort who is not above scheming against his master. The butler visits the mayor's daughter and informs her of his master's desperate plight. Together they connive to maneuver the situation into a marriage between the daughter and the marquis, but to do this, they must discredit the strange woman living in the castle who has won the affections of the marquis.

The chance to discredit Marta arrives when the miller's wife returns the necklace that Marta had given her—and returns it into the hands of the scheming butler. Playing innocent, he brings it to the marquis, telling him who returned it and why.

Furious, Sebastian goes to Marta's room and demands an explanation. Marta admits that she gave it to the peasants so that they could use it to pay their rent. In his anger, Sebastian strikes Marta and she falls to the floor in a swoon. Her bad memories of the guitarist are revived by Sebastian's conduct. That night Marta flees from the castle and makes her way towards the mountains, away from the people who have always given her grief.

The next scene opens with an eagle flying through the air. The camera tilts downward from the sky and finally settles on Marta, who is slowly climbing the mountain. Finally, she collapses in exhaustion. Not far from where she falls, Pedro is sitting in the middle of his flock, playing his flute. The music is lonely, much like the melancholy shepherd's music heard in Wagner's *Tristan und Isolde.* The sheep become increasingly disturbed. Searching for the cause of the disturbance, Pedro finds Marta. For Pedro it is the realization of his dreams, and he picks up her sleeping body and brings her to his hut.

Sebastian, in the meantime, has discovered Marta's flight and ordered his servants to find her. Two of them have followed her trail to the mountains, and already they are not far from Pedro's hut.

Marta wakes up, but she is delirious. She sees Pedro's gentle face but in her delirium Pedro's face becomes Sebastian's, contorted in an evil, demonic expression. She becomes excited, and Pedro is forced to restrain her. At that instant the door is thrown open by Sebastian's men and they carry Marta off. The protesting and bewildered Pedro is warned not to follow and to mind his own business. Nevertheless, Pedro follows the men as they bring Marta back to the lowlands and to imprisonment with the marquis.

Marta's return does not mean the end of Sebastian's problems. The mayor arrives at the castle to present the marquis with a bill, one the marquis cannot pay. Sebastian is now forced into the same position that he created for the peasants. The harvest has been bad, and Sebastian requests a year's extension of the debt. The mayor holds fast and demands his money. There is only one way out of his difficulties, the mayor grimly informs Sebastian. He must marry his daughter, and "the other must go." The temperamental Sebastian angrily orders the mayor out.

Sebastian confides to his butler that he doesn't know what to do next. The butler is quick with a solution: Sebastian should marry the mayor's daughter but keep Marta as a mistress. Marta can be married to someone in the village but only to bear his name while she remains at Sebastian's command. "That's the solution," Sebastian shouts, and runs out of the room to implement the new plan.

Sebastian visits Marta in her room. Although she never appeared to reciprocate his love, she had always been friendly to him. But Marta cannot now forget that Sebastian had struck her, and when he enters, she recoils from him in fear and hatred. Sebastian forces her into an embrace. "I need you," he tells her, "and I would rather kill you than lose you."

Pedro, having followed Marta to the lowlands, returns forlornly to his hut where the old shepherd is waiting for him. He has come to inform Pedro that, on orders of the marquis, he must leave the mountains, become the village miller, and marry Marta. At first Pedro thinks the old shepherd's words are only a cruel joke, but when he is assured they are true, he is ecstatic. Once again his dreams seem to be coming true. Pedro explains to the old shepherd that Marta is the girl of his dreams, the one he has loved since he first watched her dance in the café. The wise old shepherd is worried for Pedro, whose innocence does not give him the protection he needs from the cruelty of people in the lowlands. He warns Pedro about life below the mountains. "You don't know the lowlands, Pedro. Things are bad in the valley. The people there are different from us," but his message falls on uncomprehending ears.

Pedro, anxious to join his love and begin his new life, packs his belongings into a small bundle, takes one last look at his hut, and descends to the valley, unaware of what is awaiting him.

Marta stands in front of a mirror, clothed in a bridal dress, while busy maids scurry about her. Sebastian enters and orders the maids out of the room. "Tonight I will come to you," he tells Marta on the day of her "marriage" to Pedro.

Pedro arrives in the village. Like Junta in *The Blue Light,* he is jeered by the villagers and taunted by the little children. The puzzled Pedro does not understand their conduct but tries to ignore it.

Marta is again shown in her dressing room, a look of helplessness on her face. Earlier, when she was brought back to the castle after her flight, she had described what happened to the sympathetic housekeeper. She fondly recalls a shepherd's face from her delirium but does not know if she actually saw it or not. But now, even though she is going to be married to this young shepherd, she is not happy. She does not know that he is the shepherd she saw in her delirium, but she does know the reason for the marriage and the marquis's intentions. When Marta is informed that Pedro has arrived to see her, she refuses to let him in and sends word that he must wait for her at the church.

Pedro waits for his bride in the square in front of the church. The crowd is still taunting him, and even though it is his wedding day, he is still clad in his poor shepherd's clothing. Finally, he sees Marta at the other end of the square. She approaches him, all the time refusing to look him in the face. They enter the church together.

As soon as Pedro and Marta enter the church, the action cuts to the wedding banquet of Sebastian and the mayor's daughter. Their ceremony is over and the celebration has begun. Sebastian proposes a toast to the beauty of his new bride, dutifully acting out his part of the charade.

Marta and Pedro enter their new home, the village mill. Pedro tries to embrace her, but she breaks away. Pedro is bewildered by her actions, and asks why she won't look him in the face. "I would rather be alone. I despise you. I despise you for having the miller and his wife thrown out of here for us," Marta tells him. She does not fully understand what has happened and wrongly blames Pedro for the miller's fate. Pedro denies having anything to do with it, maintaining that his love was always tending sheep in the mountains and that he had no desire to be a miller. Marta is not convinced and continues to believe that Pedro has acted in consort with Sebastian.

Clouds gather over the mountain tops, and a fierce storm, in keeping with the events of the evening, is brewing. Spectacular shots show dark ominous clouds drifting across the mountain peaks.

While the storm gathers, a group of villagers has gathered outside the mill to continue taunting Pedro. Everyone understands what has happened, everyone, that is, except Pedro. They break open one of the mill's windows and laugh at Pedro. Angrily chasing them away, Pedro catches one of the villagers and drags him back kicking and screaming to the mill. Pedro demands that he apologize to Marta. Instead, Marta tells Pedro to let him go, and as soon as he does so, the villager renews his jeers of Pedro as he runs away. His final act is to shout "Fool!" at Pedro from the hill overlooking the mill.

Pedro demands that Marta tell him the truth, that she tell him whatever it is that everyone else seems to know. The old shepherd's warning about Pedro not understanding the people in the lowlands has come true. When Marta refuses to answer, he asks if there is someone else besides him. Marta answers yes, and the dejected Pedro walks away.

The storm has broken loose, and the fury of its winds forces open the windows at Sebastian's wedding celebration and causes panic among the guests. Breaking away from his bride, Sebastian insists that he must "tend to his cattle." Instead, however, Sebastian walks through the village towards the mill. As he feels his way through the fierce winds of the storm, he appears as a dark Mephistophelian figure.

Pedro is sitting outside the mill in the rain, his feelings hurt, trying to understand how such a happy day could have ended so miserably. Marta has had second thoughts about her conduct towards Pedro and begins to realize that he, like her, has been only a helpless pawn in Sebastian's devious game.

Marta asks him to come back into the mill. When he is reticent, she states that she no longer wants to be alone. For the first time, they embrace and kiss.

Sebastian continues to make his way toward the mill, but as he gets closer, a group of villagers clothed in black cloaks and hats start to follow him in the shadows. The time of reckoning is nearing.

Sebastian breaks into the mill, and Marta flees to the protection of Pedro's arms. "It is our wedding day," Sebastian proclaims, as he tries to wrestle Marta away from Pedro. Pedro, springing to Marta's aid, shouts "You are the wolf" at Sebastian, and a fight between the two begins as Sebastian pulls a knife. The fight is filmed in the same close-up style as Pedro's fight with the wolf in the film's opening sequence. The analogy is of course intentional, and as in other Riefenstahl films, the end brings the film back to its beginning.

During the fierce fighting, the wind blows the door of the mill open. Standing outside in a sinister and deadly line are the black-clad villagers. Despite the strength of the wind, they remain fixed in their positions, waiting for Sebastian. Their patience with his greed has reached an end.

Losing the battle with Pedro, Sebastian runs outside, only to be confronted by the villagers. Trapped between the villagers and Pedro, Sebastian returns to fight Pedro, and in a climactic ending which reflects the fight with the wolf, Pedro strangles Sebastian. A close-up shows Sebastian's lifeless body lying on the ground.

The film's final scene shows a romantic, dreamy shot of Pedro and Marta climbing the mountain, arm in arm. They are leaving the greed of Tiefland behind them and returning to the purity of the mountains.

The film was still waiting for the final editing when the end of the war brought work to a halt. All the footage for *Tiefland* was seized by the French occupying forces and impounded. When Riefenstahl finally succeeded in legally getting the film back in her possession in 1953, she discovered that the French had lost a significant amount of the completed footage. In Riefenstahl's opinion, the missing footage is some of the most important of the film. The plot can stand alone without this footage, but the ideas that Riefenstahl was trying to convey become lost, or at best muddled.

In filming *Tiefland,* Riefenstahl had several ideas in mind. One was to contrast the difference between the Hochland (highlands) and the Tiefland (lowlands) in their place in nature and their effect on humans. The Tiefland cannot exist on its own; it is a dry and barren land without the water from the Hochland. The Hochland, unlike the Tiefland, has everything it needs, and for humans, is a paradise on earth because they can escape from their fellow humans into the solitude of the mountains. The missing footage not only obscures these concepts but changes the ending of the film. When Sebastian dies and the camera films a close-up of his body, the missing footage showed raindrops slowly starting to fall into the palm of his hand. With the death of Sebastian, life returns to the lowlands. The few raindrops become a pouring rainfall, and succeeding shots depicted nature springing back to life, with water filling the irrigation ditches and life returning to the fields. None of these shots can be seen in the film today, and Riefenstahl maintains that their absence changes the tone entirely from what she had intended. For this reason, she does not like the film today and kept it out of circulation for many years. It was released in 1954 and received substantial critical acclaim, particularly in Italy where Vittorio De Sica was one of its most ardent admirers. Despite its reception, Riefenstahl allowed the film to run only until it had generated an adequate return and then withdrew it from theatrical exhibition.

Riefenstahl's personal judgment of the film is far too harsh, however, and is undoubtedly due to the fact that it took twenty years for her to complete the project, from the first attempt in 1934 to its belated release in 1954. But for someone not personally involved with the tribulations of making the film, it is exquisitely photographed, and critically, a valuable contribution to Riefenstahl's work.

Riefenstahl, playing the role of Marta, is very convincing in her acting and one can understand why she finally decided to assume the role. But the real star of the film is Franz Eichberger as Pedro, a Riefenstahl discovery who unfortunately was unable to find further acting roles after *Tiefland.* The innocence and naiveté required for his role could very easily have been overstated and overacted, but he manages to avoid this danger with a very natural performance. Although Bernhard Minetti is adequate as Sebastian, it is a pity that Riefenstahl was unable to realize her previous plan of having Heinrich George in the role. The other major contribution is in the faces of the peasants, carefully selected by Riefenstahl to show that certain quality of weathered ruggedness found in people living close to nature.

Another of Riefenstahl's intentions was to make a stand for creative monochrome. Despite the hardships resulting from losing the war, Germany, even during the war years, was diverting important chemicals and scientific labor to the film industry for the development of color stock. Movies always had a priority with the Nazi government, and the more it appeared to Propaganda Minister Goebbels that the war was being lost, the more he concentrated on films which served either as propaganda for the war effort or diversion from its hardships. With Goebbel's encouragement, color epics were pressed into production, among them *Die Goldene Stadt* (The Golden City), *Munchhausen,* and most significantly, the propaganda epic designed to instill the "werewolf" spirit in the German people, Veit Harlan's *Kolberg.* Although Riefenstahl was not hostile to color in theory, she feared that the public fascination with color would eventually cause the complete demise of black and white. She proved to be remarkably prescient in her forecast.

Tiefland was Riefenstahl's attempt to show the creative advantages that monochrome had to offer. She continued the experiments she had been conducting since *The Blue Light,* developing filters that transformed the starkness of black and white into subtle, atmospheric shadings that complemented what she was trying to express in the film. Using a special emulsion from Agfa, she was able to film outdoor settings with a painting-like quality, particularly when filming the picturesque peaks of the Dolomites. In her experimentation with emulsions, filters, and aperture settings in *Tiefland,* Riefenstahl always exercised complete control. Rushes were received each day so that she could see if the desired effects were being obtained. The exposed film was rushed by car from the Dolomites to Berlin each day for developing. With this system, Riefenstahl was able to see the film no later than three days after it was shot, which enabled her to make constant changes and improvements. The strikingly filmed exterior shots in *Tiefland* attest to the attention that Riefenstahl focused on the photography.

Critically, *Tiefland* can best be examined by comparing it with her first film, *The Blue Light.* Both films concern themselves with the same problems, and *Tiefland* can be regarded as a more mature, more fully developed continuation of the ideas initiated in the first film.

In *Tiefland,* Riefenstahl continues to contrast, this time with more emphasis than in *The Blue Light,* the purity of life in the mountains with living in society in the lowlands. This contrast is a standard trait of the mountain film genre.

The Blue Light, however, was content to deal merely with human failings: the intolerance of the villagers toward Junta and their persecution of her. But in *Tiefland,* Riefenstahl goes further than human failings and examines the failings of society: a leader who ignores the pleas of his people, who forces them into suffering for his own benefit; the injustice of a feudal system that allows one man to divert communal water for his own needs; and the peasants' inability to redress their grievances within the established system. Riefenstahl takes an established convention of the American western genre (the cattlemen versus the homesteaders) and transforms it into European social criticism, grounded in the facts of European life and history. The battle for water is only representative of the struggles of the commoners against their masters through

Europe's history, and the story could in many respects fit the twentieth century as well as the eighteenth (presumably the setting for *Tiefland*).

Drawing from characterizations found in *The Blue Light,* Riefenstahl again plays a gypsy. Marta is more integrated into society than was Junta, who was a complete outsider. Instead of being Junta's symbol of purity and innocence, however, Marta is morally ambiguous. Although she lives a life of good intentions, her exposure to the evils of the world has affected her reactions to life. Thus she can never accept Sebastian even though he loves her and can promise her a comfortable life. Nor can she bring herself to trust the innocent and well-intentioned Pedro. The true Junta role in *Tiefland* is not Marta, but Pedro. In adding more psychological motivations to her characters than was evident in *The Blue Light,* Riefenstahl reverses the sexual roles. Rather than being like Junta, Marta is reminiscent of Matias, the Viennese painter. Both have good intentions, but both are nevertheless a part of society and possess its imperfections. And though Pedro lives in the mountains apart from society like Junta, their treatment by the people in the lowlands is different. Junta is feared and scorned by the villagers, but Pedro is only mocked and laughed at.

The conflicts in both films not only revolve around the imperfections of man and society but around threats posed by nature. In *The Blue Light,* the threat is the mysterious blue light emanating from Mount Cristallo. It is a benevolent threat; it is only dangerous because human curiosity has made it so. Its origins, however, are still in nature. The threat from nature in *Tiefland* is more plain: it is the lack of water in the lowlands, further complicated by Sebastian's refusal to share it. The threat in each film lies in nature, and a human being holds the key to the threat. And in each film, the human being who holds the key perishes through the actions of fellow humans: Junta in *The Blue Light* and Sebastian in *Tiefland*.

The major difference between the two films is in their endings. *Tiefland* ends happily with the uniting of Marta and

Pedro and their ascent into the mountains away from the lowlands. *The Blue Light* ends in tragedy with the separation of the two lovers through the death of Junta. *The Blue Light* was a romanticized legend, and a tragic ending is in keeping with the atmosphere of the legend. But *Tiefland,* intended as social comment without any legendary basis, requires an ending that is consistent with the theme of the film: the triumph of purity.

CHAPTER V

OLYMPIA FILM AND LENI RIEFENSTAHL FILM

An obscure area of Riefenstahl's work in films which merits study is the output of her two production companies, Olympia Film and Leni Riefenstahl Film. Although Riefenstahl did not make the films herself, they were filmed by her personally trained protégés and bear both the names of her production companies and the mark of her influence.

When Riefenstahl finally completed the editing of *Olympia,* she had not only a large team of cameramen, cutters, and other helpers in her employ but also a mountain of unused footage. Just as Dr. Fanck had helped school his early assistants in the 1920's, Riefenstahl decided that the unused footage would be used by her young assistants as an opportunity to work with filmmaking on their own. She allowed them to experiment with the footage, making *Kulturfilme* (cultural films) and short films to be played before the feature attraction in German theaters. Riefenstahl insists that in the production of these films, their makers were completely unsupervised and that she played no role in their assembly.

Four films are known to have been made from the outtakes from *Olympia.* They are *Höchstes Glück der Erde auf dem Rücken der Pferde* (The Greatest Happiness in the World—on the Back of a Horse), *Kraft und Schwung* (Strength and Energy), *Schwimmen und Springen* (Swimming and Diving), and *Der Wurf im Sport* (The Discus in Sport). Of these four films, only one, *Höchstes Glück der Erde auf dem Rücken der Pferde,* is still preserved today in the German Federal Film Archives. It is also the only one of the four to be mentioned in the film trade papers of the time. The others have disappeared.

Assembled by Joachim Bartsch, later to be credited with helping Riefenstahl script her unrealized film *Die Roten Teufel* (The Red Devils), *Höchstes Glück der Erde* is taken from the equestrian competition footage, along with additional footage shot later. Bartsch's commentary for the film manages to underline concepts of athletic superiority to a ludicrous extreme. Opening a book on horses, the film's narrator notes that "Every horse has a special destiny." These words are followed by shots of workhorses pulling plows in the fields, followed by horses on the next level of "respectability," the carriage horse, pulling carriages along the roads. And then the narrator adds, "Only a few are born to be *racing horses!*" With mention of the racing horses, there are shots of these "elitest" horses jumping and training. As a shot shows a Wehrmacht officer on the back of one of the racing horses, the announcer notes that the horse "is proud to carry the officer on his back." The film continues with more shots of the horses training in the stadium. On its release in early 1940, a film trade magazine reported that "This pretty and fascinating *Kulturfilm,* interestingly narrated by Jochen Poelzig, received spontaneous applause from the audience."[1] Knowing the effusive nature of German film trade magazines, it is easy to speculate that it was the horses, not the film, receiving the applause.

Two other films were produced by Olympia Film before the company stopped production. *Osterskitour in Tyrol* was a short about an Easter skiing trip through the Tyrolean mountains. The second was entitled *Wildwasser* and was the first film to be made by Guzzi Lantschner, who had been a cameraman for *Olympia. Wildwasser* was co-directed by Harald Reinl, who later served as co-director of *Tiefland.*[2] The film was the story of a kayak trip down river rapids by the two co-directors, and enough excitement was generated to win the approval of the trade magazines. The film was undoubtedly aided by a musical score composed by Herbert Windt.

With the exhaustion of the *Olympia* material and the outbreak of war in 1939, production work shifted from Olympia Film to Leni Riefenstahl Film. Early in the war, Riefenstahl was approached by her old friend Albert Speer to make a film about his architecture. Besides designing the structures at the Party Rally grounds in Nuremberg, Speer was also responsible for the extravagant Chancellery building designed for Hitler in Berlin. Hitler's plans for Speer and his architecture included the rebuilding of Berlin into an "Imperial City," crowned with a massive domed hall and triumphal arch.[3] Since she had already completed two documentaries, Riefenstahl was not interested in working in the relatively tedious field of *Kulturfilme*. When Speer insisted that he wanted only an artist of stature to film his work, Riefenstahl suggested a compromise. She would delegate the work to Dr. Arnold Fanck, who was by then an employee of Leni Riefenstahl Film, while she, as his supervisor, would be able to exercise any necessary artistic control. To accommodate this arrangement, a new department was established within the corporate structure of Leni Riefenstahl Film known as the "Abteilung Organisation Todt" (Organization Todt Department). The Organisation Todt was Speer's ministry, an all-encompassing body responsible for all major building projects in the Third Reich, from the designing of government buildings to the construction of railroads, highways, defense systems, and fortifications. The new department's activities would be financed through funds received from the Organisation Todt (OT). Through this arrangement, Leni Riefenstahl Film became a subcontractor of the German government, operating independently but working on government projects financed with government capital.

Correspondence found in archives shows that this special arrangement continued to the final days of the war. One letter, dated March 1, 1945, indicates that a director named Richard Scheinpflug was still working on a commission for a film about the history of the Organisation Todt, to be assembled from film clips in the Organisation Todt film archives.[4]

Dr. Fanck's association with Leni Riefenstahl Film is an intriguing story of declining fortunes. After leaving the mountain film genre in 1934, Fanck found that his success in mountain films could not be carried over to other genres. His own directorial career ended with two failures, a curious German-Japanese co-production in 1936 entitled *Die Tochter des Samurai* (The Daughter of the Samurai) and a 1939 Robinson Crusoe film entitled *Ein Robinson—das Tagebuch eines Matrosen* (Robinson Crusoe—Diary of a Sailor). Unable to find work elsewhere, he went to his early discovery, Leni Riefenstahl.[5]

Fanck began a film about Speer's plans for the rebuilding of Berlin, but according to Walter Traut, the production chief of Leni Riefenstahl Film, it was never completed.[6] Some footage was shot using Speer's construction models, mounted in a Berlin studio, of the major buildings to be constructed.

Fanck did make several other *Kulturfilme* for Leni Riefenstahl Film, including films about the sculptures of such Nazi favorites as Arno Breker, Thorak, Klimsch, and Ambrosi, and a film about the quarrying of marble in the quarries of Carara.

One of these films, *Arno Breker,* is preserved in the Federal Film Archives. The credits list Dr. Fanck as the director, script and editing by Dr. Hans Kurlis, photography by Walter Riml, and music by Rudolf Perak. The film opens with a view of the new Chancellery courtyard in Berlin, which featured two of Breker's most famous statues, "The Party" and "The Army." The statues are of nude athletic male figures done in Breker's characteristic heroic style. The camera studies the statues in the same slow tracking style that Riefenstahl used to study the ancient Greek statuary in the prologue of *Olympia.* The teacher has become the student of the pupil, and the camera work and editing is all definitely in the Riefenstahl style. The film follows Breker at work in his huge Berlin studio, working on the nudes, eagles, horses, and busts of

Wagner preferred by the Nazis. The film also follows the creation of the statue "Kameradschaft," from Breker's rough sketch from a model to preparation of the clay miniature. As Fanck observed about these short films in his memoirs, "The photography was good, but the films were nothing special."[7] *Arno Breker* remains significant today only as a record of works that today no longer survive.[8]

Besides Fanck's work for Leni Riefenstahl Film, other camera teams produced a film about the Westwall, the German defense fortifications constructed opposite the French Maginot Line. Other footage was shot by teams accompanying Speer to the front to inspect fortifications, but what films emerged from those efforts seem to be lost today.

Although Riefenstahl cannot be personally credited with these films, they are the products of her production companies and reflect the realities of the preoccupations of a nation at war.

CHAPTER VI

PENTHESILEA

The world of filmmaking is as much a world of unfulfilled dreams as it is of completed films. Also, the filmmaker faces an artistic hardship not known to the author or painter. A painter can paint a canvas and the author can write a book, and their artistic urges will have borne fruit. But the filmmaker, working in an expensive art form grounded in the commercial facts of life, cannot always realize the films visualized in the mind's eye. Many potential classics have never been filmed because of failure to obtain the necessary financial backing.

While *Triumph of the Will* and *Olympia* stand as classics of documentary film, Riefenstahl's two fiction films, *The Blue Light* and *Tiefland* have been critically neglected. But they are intimations of the flair that Riefenstahl had for feature films as well as documentaries, and it should be kept in mind that for Riefenstahl, both films were preliminaries for the project that she saw as her life's work: the filming of Heinrich von Kleist's play, *Penthesilea.*

In studying Riefenstahl's plans for *Penthesilea,* the single source of information is Riefenstahl herself. Since the project was never realized, it remains today only what it has always been: an idea in her mind. A filmmaker's hoped for but never realized projects can be as important as the completed films. They reveal the interests and aspirations of the artist and point to directions that might have been followed had the artist's fortunes fared better. World War II put an end to Riefenstahl's hopes for filming *Penthesilea,* but the remains of her shattered dreams suggest a film that could very well have crowned her career.

Riefenstahl wanted to film *Penthesilea* for many reasons, but the most important was what the play meant to her personally:

> In 1926 I read *Penthesilea* for the first time. It became an unforgettable, intense experience. Since then I love Kleist as I love no other poet and dramatist. I feel myself so akin to him that in no place in his poetic work do I ever stray from his feelings—everything is spoken from the depths of my soul. In *Penthesilea* I found my own individuality as in no other character. When I read *Penthesilea* for the first time, the effect was so strong that I was deeply moved for days, indeed for weeks. And from this experience there grew the wish to reproduce *Penthesilea*.[1]

It was an experience rivaling that day in Berlin when she saw her first mountain film, an experience that awakened the artistic and adventurous impulses in her. She also saw the play as a chance to introduce to the German and international public a writer she felt had been too long neglected.

Riefenstahl was further attracted to the classical setting of this tale of the Amazon Queen Penthesilea and the Greek hero Achilles. Her fondness for antiquity has always been pronounced, as is evident in the prologue of *Olympia*. Riefenstahl has always regarded her own learnings as being closer to antiquity than to any other period of human history.[2] In *Olympia,* her camera treats the human body with the same care as an ancient sculptor; indeed, Riefenstahl brings the famous "discus thrower" statue to life in her film, sculpting with the camera just as her Greek counterparts had done in their own age with their own art. And with *Penthesilea,* Riefenstahl wanted to bring the time, as well as its art, back to life.

Riefenstahl had decided to film *Penthesilea* long before she made *Olympia*. But her reverence for the project was so great at that moment in her artistic development that she did not feel ready to attempt it. *Penthesilea* was to mean for her career what *The Ring of the Nibelungs* meant for Wagner's: a *Gesamtkunstwerk* of the cinema. It was to recognize the full potential of film, bringing into its service all elements that together make film art: the interplay of movement, atmosphere, dialogue, and music. As Riefenstahl explained her concept:

> Film will become art only when—by the means that are possible only in film—it creates the artistic experience that no other art can give us: the harmonious fusion of optical, acoustical, rhythmical and architectonic factors—then film will become the king of the arts.[3]

Olympia gave Riefenstahl the experience and the confidence to attempt such an elevated ideal of the cinema, and after it was completed, she devoted her energies to *Penthesilea*. By 1939, the script had been written, locations selected, and one hundred carefully selected young women were in Libya learning the skills of horseback riding in preparation for their roles as Amazons. Riefenstahl, who had always envisioned herself playing the role of Penthesilea, was also in training for what she knew would be the most difficult acting challenge of her career.

The major artistic question facing Riefenstahl was how to transfer Kleist's play to the screen while still remaining true to the author. As much as possible, she wanted to *film* Kleist rather than make a film *based* on Kleist. The problem did not appear difficult to her since, in her opinion, the play had been written for the screen and not for the stage. If Kleist had lived in contemporary times, it would certainly have been a screenplay rather than a stage play; Kleist was merely working under the limitations of his times. And since it was ill-suited for the stage, the play was rarely performed. The scope of the play is epic, covering huge battle scenes that could never be performed convincingly on the stage. As Riefenstahl observed, it is convincing only as a radio play where the visuals can be forgotten and left to the minds of the listeners, or as a film.

For *The Blue Light,* Riefenstahl felt that a legendary story had to be told in a fantasized setting that transcends reality. In attempting to film Kleist's play while keeping his poetic language intact, Riefenstahl was also confronted with the problem of how to translate a legendary story with non-realistic, poetic dialogue to the inherently realistic medium of the cinema.

To Riefenstahl, although the recording nature of film is grounded in realism, the creative interference of the artist may mold the medium in any direction chosen, and for Riefenstahl, the chosen direction was stylized fantasy.

Keeping Kleist's poetic dialogue or making it more realistic was never a choice for Riefenstahl. The dialogue had to be used not only because of her admiration for Kleist but because she felt Kleist's poetry to be the height of perfection, and any attempt to produce new dialogue would be egoistic idiocy. But how would the poetry sound on the screen? The example of the film *Der Zerbrochene Krug* was always cited to Riefenstahl by those who felt that poetry could not be successfully used on the motion picture screen. *Der Zerbrochene Krug,* starring the famous Emil Jannings, was a previous attempt to film Kleist's poetry. It was more of a film of the stage play than a film itself and used all of the original script. Audiences reacted very negatively to the bulky Jannings speaking in verse, and the film was a failure. But Riefenstahl welcomed the comparison with *Der Zerbrochene Krug* and used it as a reinforcement of her own arguments. *Der Zerbrochene Krug,* she argued, had a realistic setting. The film opens with a realistic room, with a man lying in bed. He wakes up, blows his nose, and walks around in a realistic manner. All of what is happening is a scene from everyday life. But then he starts to speak in verse. Of course the audience will reject the film, Riefenstahl pointed out, because when a realistic setting is presented in a film, one expects the realism to extend throughout. In a play the audience is accustomed to actors speaking in verse, but not in the cinema. But when a film is opened in a stylized, fantasized manner with no pretensions of reality, the audience will accept what is presented to them, including dialogue in verse. In fact, she conceived the film to be so stylized in all its facets that to have realistic dialogue would be a breach of style. When an audience is given characters from antiquity, and particularly heroic characters such as Achilles and Penthesilea, they are not expected to speak in a contemporary manner and the audience will not accept normal conversation from them.

Nevertheless, Riefenstahl planned to venture cautiously into the stylization and not start the film immediately with verse. She decided to open the film with a prologue in which no dialogue would be spoken and the burden would be placed on the combined power of the visuals and the music. In all her films, Riefenstahl has tried to avoid speech in the first ten to fifteen minutes of the film. The prologue would be used to keep the dramaturgy of Kleist's play intact. The prologue would be Riefenstahl's and would contain everything that Riefenstahl wanted to show but was not in Kleist's work, or was only narrated in the play. The Amazon state and its city of Thermiscyra would be introduced. The characters of Penthesilea and Achilles would also be defined, for the sake of economy later in the film. The heroic nature of Achilles would be developed by borrowing a scene from *The Iliad.* Achilles, in great anguish because his closest friend Patroclus has been slain by Hector, would be shown exacting his revenge by dragging the dead body of Hector, tied to his chariot, around the funeral pyre of his friend. But after the prologue, the poetry and drama of Kleist would take over.

Riefenstahl was careful, however, to avoid merely attempting to film Kleist's play as it was written. Recognizing the power of the cinema, she realized that some of Kleist's beautiful language could best be presented visually rather than verbally, and therefore Kleist's play would be shortened and strengthened through the addition of visuals that followed the sense of his poetry. As Riefenstahl wrote, the key to the dialogue "will be to leave out that which can be shown visually with at least equal force."[4]

The film would not be dependent merely on dialogue for its stylization and departure from reality. The movements and gestures of the actors were to be stylized as well, setting off their differences from modern players. Their clothing would be as simple and basic as possible, imitating the manner of Greek statues where the clothing merely drapes the body, serving to accentuate rather than hide the contours of the human form.

Although Riefenstahl attempted to make a stand for the artistic use of monochrome in *Tiefland*, she was not theoretically opposed to the use of color and planned to film *Penthesilea* in color. But where most early color films used color as an attempt to heighten realism, Riefenstahl's intention was to use it as yet another device to set the film apart from reality. Color was to be used sparsely rather than elaborately, and she hoped to use subtle shades of color to create a hued stone-like effect. She would apply the same experimentations in filters and emulsions to color that she had done in black and white.

Not a single scene was to be realistically photographed. Even the battle scenes were to be filmed in such a way that they appeared much like the ancient Greek bas-reliefs. They were to be filmed against a cloudless blue sky with a filter, resulting in a greyish tone on the battlefield. This would be the reverse of the *Olympia* prologue situation; instead of bringing statues to life, she would convert life into statues.

The most significant change in Riefenstahl's approach was her decision to stylize nature as well. She would not only use nature, as she had done in *The Blue Light* and *Tiefland*, but would add to it. Sets would be constructed within natural surroundings that would provide Riefenstahl with the effects she desired which were not readily available in nature. She noted:

> Everything is to be taken directly from nature. Nevertheless, very much will have to be constructed in this film, because the natural setting must be enhanced: foreground, perspective, trees and rocks must be as

moveable as is necessary for the composition of the
picture. To be sure, everything is to be found in nature,
but then one would have to search in the world with our
actors for years, until we have found all the motifs that
agree with our conception. Therefore, the construction
of sets will probably be combined with natural surroundings.[5]

In the writings that Riefenstahl made in preparation for
Penthesilea are found her major explicit statements on the
nature of the cinema. Apart from the writings, her views have
been articulated only in the numerous interviews she has
given film scholars over the years. Consequently, her notes in
preparation for *Penthesilea* increase in importance as a tool for
understanding her work. In wrestling with the problems that
confronted her, Riefenstahl raises the critical issues that are at
the heart of her work up to *Penthesilea:* the stylization of
reality, and how to use the realistic medium of the cinema to
present something more than reality.

Had *Penthesilea* been filmed, it would have been the first
time that Riefenstahl tampered with nature before the
filming; for her other films, the stylization was not through
the sets but through the photography and the editing. As she
observed about *The Blue Light:*

In my first film, *The Blue Light,* I attempted . . . to
photograph nature without any help of stylized sets, so
that the film had, from the first to the last frame, along
with the people acting in them, an unreal, fabulous,
stylized effect. And I succeeded in this already at that
time. My walls of rock looked different from how they
did in the Alpine films, in spite of the fact that they were
the same rocks. My country folk looked different from
those in the *Bauernspielfilme.*[6]

Thus the word "stylized," or more precisely, "stylized
reality," becomes the key to understanding Riefenstahl's
approach to the cinema. Riefenstahl takes the material of
reality: rocks, mountains, trees, people, and using this
material, she shapes reality until it transcends itself. Camera

placements, selection of settings, the use of varying emulsions, lights, and filters are her instruments of stylization. The
peasant faces in *The Blue Light* and *Tiefland* are real peasant
faces, but through Riefenstahl's careful selection (much like
Eisenstein's typing but more realistic), they become more
representations than individuals. The same is true of the
previously noted "statues on film" technique in *Triumph of
the Will*. The faces of the young Germans are selected from
the fabric of reality, the crowds that were actually present at
the events, but through Riefenstahl's camera they become
more than individuals in the crowd; they are an idealized
representation.

This stylization of reality is pronounced in all her films,
from the example given above to *Tiefland*. A shot of Pedro in
Tiefland standing on the mountaintop amid his sheep has a
dreamy, unrealistic aura, yet it is not a studio shot. It is
actually filmed in the mountains, with nothing artificially
added to nature but created through special emulsions. In the
same manner, the entrance of Nazi flags in *Triumph of the
Will* becomes more than the reality of the event; it is a
stunningly composed shot of inanimate objects seemingly
possessing a life of their own.

Penthesilea highlights an artistic concern found throughout
Riefenstahl's films: the beauty of the human body, and the
body's beauty enhanced through movement. Not since
Muybridge has the cinema been so preoccupied with this
subject, and it is undoubtedly the result of Riefenstahl's
earlier career as a dancer. Anyone who can master that
particularly demanding art form must have instilled within an
appreciation of the grace of the human body.

Indeed, all of Riefenstahl's films are dominated by two
concerns: either the beauty of nature and physical surroundings, or the beauty of the human body, and, as a corollary, the
beauty of the body in movement, either single (as in *Olympia*)
or in mass (as in *Triumph of the Will*).

Penthesilea was to continue Riefenstahl's search for beauty.
As she noted:

> The beauty of the body, the stature of the human
> being created by God, shall receive its rightful recogni-
> tion in this film as in no other until now. Just as Kleist's
> language is an ecstasy of beauty, so the human bodies in
> this film must portray an ecstasy of bodily beauty. Every
> thigh, every arm, every neck must be beautiful—
> beautiful, not in the ordinary sense of a popularized sort
> of beauty,—but beautiful as Michelangelo created his
> sculptures—beautiful, just as everything in creation.[7]

The beauty of the bodies would again be emphasized
through movement as well as appearance. Particularly in the
battle scenes, which Riefenstahl envisioned as strange atmospheric events transpiring in whirling clouds of fog and dust,
the bodies of the actors and actresses would assume their
most heroic roles, and so would their horses:

> During the battle scenes one must often see in
> close-up the sweating bodies of the horses—the bodies
> of horses that are being spurred on to utmost perfor-
> mance by the naked legs of the women.[8]

Penthesilea was to have four sets: the city of Thermiscyra, a
section of the wall near Troy, the Greek camp, and the camp
of the Amazons. As inspiration for the set designs, Riefenstahl was prepared to comb art history; she lists sources which
included reconstructions of the ancient Greek cities as they
actually appeared (found in Holt-Hofmannsthal's *Greece*);
stage and film sets from Max Reinhardt and Fritz Lang; and
works by impressionistic, expressionistic, and modern paint-
ers. The art designs were to concentrate heavily on the
mythology of the time, and particularly that of the Amazons.
During the prologue, the moon would appear as a symbol,
and certain key scenes would be filmed in moonlight, all to
accentuate the moon culture of the Amazons. The film would
also emphasize other celestial motifs.
Although Riefenstahl completed the script, it has long
since been lost. However, Riefenstahl delineates the thirty-
four major scenes contained in Kleist's Penthesilea, either

directly on the stage or narrated, in her production notes, which she saw as an action outline for her film. The scenes, along with the capsule summaries of the action, give an indication of the scope she envisaged for the film:

1. The Amazons attack the Trojans in battle.
2. The Greeks decide to offer the Amazons an alliance. Achilles and Odysseus go to meet Penthesilea; the first meeting; Penthesilea refuses the alliance.
3. The great battle of the Amazons against the Greeks and the Trojans.
4. Penthesilea spares Achilles' life in the battle.
5. Achilles' chariot crashes; Penthesilea and the Amazons block his way. Penthesilea plunges from a crag on her horse, but without injury. Then, along with her Amazons, she pursues the fleeing Achilles.
6. Penthesilea pursues Achilles; Achilles tricks her, pulls his horse and chariot around; Penthesilea and the Amazons following her fall down violently.
7. Achilles in camp.
8. With the Amazons, a pause in battle. Penthesilea with Prothoe, Asteria, Meroe. Prothoe tries to keep Penthesilea from continuing the battle with Achilles.
9. New attack by the Amazons against the Greeks; great battle scenes.
10. While she is pursuing Achilles, Penthesilea directs the High Priestess to start the rose festival.
11. The Rose Festival: the High Priestess, priestesses, rose maidens, captured Greeks, armed Amazons.
12. The Amazon captain reports to the High Priestess concerning the battle. She reports that Penthesilea has fallen in love with Achilles. High Priestess sends an Amazon into the field of battle with a message for Penthesilea.
13. The battlefield—Achilles and Penthesilea engage in a contest.
14. The Amazon sent by the Priestess cannot find Penthe-

silea in the turmoil of battle and brings the message to Prothoe.

15. Combat scenes between the Greeks and the Amazons.
16. The Amazon brings Prothoe's answer to the High Priestess.
17. Combat scenes; Achilles is victorious over Penthesilea.
18. An Amazon colonel, who comes out of battle, reports to the High Priestess that Penthesilea has fallen and that the army of the Greeks is rushing up.
19. Penthesilea, led by Prothoe and Meroe, comes to the place where the preceding scenes with the High Priestess took place. Penthesilea's great scene of despair—she does not want to flee and wants to plunge into the Scamander.
20. Achilles and the Amazons. Penthesilea, who has fainted, is unaware of what is happening around her. A short struggle between the Greeks and the Amazons. An Amazon who takes aim at Achilles is killed by a Greek.
21. Odysseus and Diomedes appear with Greek warriors. Achilles sends them away with the order to annihilate the fleeing army of the Amazons.
22. The great love scene between Penthesilea and Achilles.
23. The captain brings Achilles the news that the tide of battle has turned, that the army of the Amazons is advancing in order to free Penthesilea.
24. Diomedes and Odysseus appear with the Greek Army and want to take Achilles along. Achilles tries to drag Penthesilea with him.
25. Amazons throw themselves between Achilles and Penthesilea, separate them, threaten the life of Achilles who is forcibly carried away by Odysseus.
26. Penthesilea and the Amazons, without the Greeks: the High Priestess with her Priestesses appears, Penthesilea berates the Amazons for having freed her and separated her from Achilles.

27. The herald brings Penthesilea the message that Achilles is challenging Penthesilea to a new combat.
28. Achilles in the Greek camp; Odysseus and Diomedes try to prevent the combat with Penthesilea.
29. The mighty army of the Amazons on the march.
30. The Amazons throw themselves before Penthesilea, who has gone mad, rides over them and drives them away with her dogs. She throws a stone at the High Priestess, rages among the dogs.
31. The High Priestess sends for ropes in order to have Penthesilea bound.
32. Penthesilea kills Achilles.
33. An Amazon and Meroe report to the High Priestess how Penthesilea murdered Achilles.
34. Penthesilea's return to reality; Penthesilea's death.[9]

Penthesilea was Riefenstahl's most ambitious undertaking. Unfortunately, it was too ambitious for a country going to war. When the war started, all work on *Penthesilea* stopped, and Riefenstahl's hope for making her most important film ended.

CHAPTER VII

UNREALIZED FILMS

Penthesilea was not Riefenstahl's only unrealized project. There is an interesting array of others, ranging in degree of completion from mere ideas to fully arranged productions, with a finished script, signed acting contracts, and rented studios. Together, they form a long record of dashed hopes and dreams that would daunt the most optimistic of personalities.

Riefenstahl's first taste of the vagaries of the world of film production came when her ambitions still leaned more toward acting than directing. Looking about for suitable acting roles, she was offered the lead role in a film planned by Ufa entitled *Mademoiselle Docteur*. The film was based on the legendary exploits of a famous German spy during World War I, a beautiful young lady who was the nemesis of the French espionage corps. Riefenstahl was already acquainted with the adventures of the female master spy through stories told to her by Dr. Fanck, who had worked with her during the war.[1] At the time of the project, Riefenstahl was under contract to Ufa, though only as an actress.[2]

The script was written, Hans Schneeberger was signed as cameraman and G. W. Pabst as director. But then, in the summer of 1933, Ufa received word from the government that the film would not be permitted and production stopped immediately. The ruling, it was later learned, was not against the film in particular, but against all espionage films in general. The Wehrmacht Ministry was afraid that the films would reveal too much about the workings of espionage, and so all films in the genre were met with an official *Verbot*.

In 1936, Pabst resumed the project in France but without Leni Riefenstahl. *Mademoiselle Docteur* was filmed with a new script and with Dita Parlo in the leading role.

During a lull in the wartime filming of *Tiefland*, Riefenstahl had the idea to make a film about Vincent Van Gogh. The theme of the film was to be "How a genius expresses himself."[3] Riefenstahl was again preoccupied with the artistic uses of monochrome and color in cinema. Her plan was to have the dramatic scenes filmed in black and white, while the scenes that depicted how a painting is brought to life would be filmed in color. The color would be used to enhance the miracle of creativity. But like so many other wartime plans, *Van Gogh* was never developed beyond the idea stage.

By 1954, Riefenstahl had assembled *Tiefland* and the film was enjoying a successful release. With its popularity and a successful re-release of *The Blue Light* just two years earlier, it appeared to Riefenstahl that this was the opportune moment to launch her career anew. The two films were especially popular in Austria and Italy, and Riefenstahl initiated contacts for a German-Austrian-Italian coproduction. She had an idea in mind and was ready to make her first major effort to resume filmmaking since the war.

The project was to be a film entitled *Die Roten Teufel* (The Red Devils). It was to be a complete change for Riefenstahl— her first comedy. Returning once again to the mountains, *The Red Devils* was to be a frivolous skiing comedy. "The Red Devils" were an internationally famous Tyrolean skiing team, and the film concerned their competition with a Norwegian women's team and an Italian men's team.

As Riefenstahl envisaged it, *The Red Devils* would be the first skiing film to be filmed in color. The idea for the film had occurred twenty years previous, during the filming of Fanck's *Storm over the Montblanc*. One day she happened to observe a Tyrolean student ski team sweeping down the slopes of the mountain, and she was struck by the interplay of colors produced by the Tyroleans clad in red skiing sweaters speeding down the white snow-covered slopes against a clear blue sky. She realized then that a true skiing film must wait for color. The thought remained in Riefenstahl's mind, cataloged until the day that color equipment would make it possible. The idea had to wait even after the entry of the American technicolor process because the heavy cameras required by the process were not suited for the mountain slopes. Riefenstahl needed lightweight cameras that could be carried by cameramen on skis.

After a busy series of meetings in the countries involved, Riefenstahl finally put together the financial backing to make the tri-national coproduction possible. Four different versions were planned: German, Italian, French, and to carry Riefenstahl's experimentations beyond the realm of color, a 3-D version.[4] Location shots were selected at Garmisch-Partenkirchen, Lech am Arlberg, Kitzbühel, Gastein, and Cervinia on the southern slope of the Matterhorn, using its cable car, which was then the world's highest. After reading the completed script, the Italian scriptwriter Cesare Zavattini (*Bicycle Thieves, Umberto D*) was so impressed that he arranged to have his close friend and collaborator, Vittorio De Sica, play one of the lead roles.[5] On the advice of Riefenstahl's close friend, Jean Cocteau, a then unknown French actress named Brigitte Bardot was signed to play another lead role.

Two previous collaborators of Riefenstahl's, Dr. Harald Reinl and Joachim Bartsch, had written the script. Casting was completed, studios were rented, and everything was ready for filming. It had been hard work, but Riefenstahl was now on the threshold of resuming her stalled career.

Riefenstahl had realized by then that she would never be able to film *Penthesilea,* but it continued to be a source of inspiration for her. *The Red Devils* was actually *Penthesilea* transposed from an ancient Greek tragedy to a modern skiing comedy; the conflict between the Greeks and the Amazons, the love between Achilles and Penthesilea, became a battle of the sexes at the International Winter Olympics. The Amazons were transformed into a Norwegian women's skiing team, every bit as agile and athletic as the legendary Amazons, and Penthesilea became the team's captain, Christa. The Greeks were likewise transformed into a Tyrolean men's team, and Achilles became their captain, Michael. As Riefenstahl wrote in her treatment for the film:

> Like Penthesilea, the Queen of the Amazons, Christa believes herself to be invulnerable as far as love is concerned and regards men with a superior and contemptuous air until she loses her heart to Michael, the skiing champion, just as Penthesilea lost her heart to Achilles. . . . During the week of the international winter sports contest in St. Paradiso, a famous skiing paradise, a fierce but nevertheless merry war is waged by the Red Devils and the skiing Amazons.[6]

Building on her original concept, Riefenstahl wanted to use color not only to capture the beauty of the mountain scenery, but for dramatic effect as well. Since *The Red Devils* was to be the first skiing film in color, it could overcome the problem of all black-and-white skiing films: character identification on the white slopes. Riefenstahl would overcome this problem by assigning color themes to the major actors and teams. The Tyrolean team led by Michael would be clad in red (hence "The Red Devils"), which Riefenstahl regarded as a masculine color; Christa's team would be clad in blue, Riefenstahl's idea of a feminine color; and the competing Italians would be in yellow.

Riefenstahl also planned to play carefully selected rhythmic melodies over loudspeakers during the filming so that the actors and actresses could ski to the melodies, "thus giving the impression of actually dancing and gliding on their skis, an effect which will greatly emphasize the beauty of their movements."[7] In *Olympia,* Riefenstahl created such rhythmic movements mainly through editing; now she would attempt to do it during the actual filming.

The movement of the skiers, buttressed by the coordinated music, would combine with the play of colors to form what

Riefenstahl hopefully referred to as "a symphony of color, music, and movement."[8]

The rather loosely constructed plot of *The Red Devils* saw a spirited rivalry develop between the Tyrolean Reds and the Norwegian women, with both teams choosing to live in rugged training huts high on the mountain slopes rather than in the plush accommodations of St. Paradiso. A series of raids against each other's huts, along with good-natured pranks in the snow, finally leads to a skiing challenge between the two teams, and the famous battle between the Greeks and the Amazons becomes a fierce race down the slope of the mountain. Later, when the international competition begins, both Michael and Christa establish themselves as the true leaders of their teams, breaking all international records. Despite their feigned indifference to each other, Michael and Christa are in love. The ending of the film sees the two finally facing reality and accepting their love, to the delight of their teams.

Riefenstahl planned to deal once again with the theme of the purity of life in the mountains versus the corrupting habits of society below, only this time to deal with it comically. She created the character of Mr. O'Harris, a soft American tourist weakened by the ways of society, who falls in love with one of the Norwegian skiers but is unable to keep up with her athletic antics.

Riefenstahl also hoped to continue the international flavor of *Olympia* through emphasizing the international nature of the winter games that form the backdrop of the film. She wrote in her treatment:

> The film will show us not only Americans, Germans, Austrians, Norwegians, Swiss, Frenchmen, and Italians, but also Japanese, Indians, and other Orientals. Like the Winter Olympics in St. Moritz, the contests are the meeting place for the international sports world. The name, St. Paradiso, has been chosen intentionally so that shooting of the film would not have to be limited to any one of the famous winter sports resorts.[9]

Riefenstahl devoted two years to the project, only to watch events beyond her control cause it to collapse. The reasons, according to Riefenstahl, were political ones; she claims she was used as a pawn in internal Austrian politics. At the time of the production preparations, Austria was governed by a conservative government faced with a vocal leftist opposition. The opposition press, adding to reports that first appeared in Italian communist newspapers that "one of Hitler's favorites was about to resume filmmaking," started printing rumors that the Austrian government was secretly providing financing for the film. In the midst of all the accusations and denials between the government and the opposition, the worried financial backers withdrew their funds. The collapse of the project, for which she had expended so much time and energy in hopes of refurbishing her image, was a severe blow to Riefenstahl.

Several other ideas for films occupied Riefenstahl during the 1950's and early 1960's, attesting both to her indefatigable energy and wide-ranging interests. Most of these ideas, however, never went beyond the treatment stage.

One idea was for another mountain film to be entitled *Die Ewige Gipfel* (The Eternal Summit). It was to be an international film with five different chapters, filmed as a documentary. Each chapter concerned the climbing of a major summit in a different part of the world, showing the similarities in human aspirations around the world. The settings were to be Mont Blanc in France, the Matterhorn in Switzerland, the Austrian Dolomites, the Eigerwand, and as the culmination, the Himalayas.

Another idea was a film with religious overtones to be entitled *Die Drei Sterne am Mantel der Madonna* (The Three Stars on the Cloak of the Madonna). The film was intended to be a vehicle for the Italian actress Anna Magnani, who was to play a mother with three sons. During the course of the film she loses her sons, one by one, and as each one dies, she sews a star on her coat. But Magnani was not interested in the role, feeling that she was too young to play a mother of grown sons.

Drawing upon her own experiences as a dancer, Riefenstahl had an idea for a film tentatively titled *Tänzer von Florence* (The Dancer of Florence). Written only as a treatment, it chronicled the life of the famous modernist dancer Harald Kreuzberg, with whom Riefenstahl had performed as a young dancer in Berlin.

Of her unrealized films, probably the most artistically interesting is one that was to be a collaboration between Riefenstahl and the French director Jean Cocteau, to be entitled *Friedrich und Voltaire* (Frederick and Voltaire). Long an admirer of Riefenstahl's work, Cocteau had unsuccessfully attempted to have *Tiefland* entered in the 1954 Cannes Film Festival. Cocteau wanted to act in a film under Riefenstahl's direction, and proposed a film about the love-hate relationship between Frederick the Great and the French philosopher Voltaire. Cocteau would play both roles, and the theme of the film was to be the love-hate relationship of the German and French people, symbolically represented in the figures of Frederick and Voltaire. Riefenstahl and Cocteau gathered historical material and anecdotes and together wrote the treatment. Cocteau's bad health and failure to find financing doomed the project.

In 1960, Riefenstahl was approached by an English firm, Adventure Ltd. of London, to remake *The Blue Light*. The remake was to be completely different from the original and was envisioned as a ballet-fairy tale, filmed in color. Riefenstahl collaborated on a new script, but once it was completed, the project had reached an end and the film was never made.

Of all these ideas for films, one did come close to realization. A sleepless night and a chance reading of Ernest Hemingway's *The Green Hills of Africa* inspired Riefenstahl with an interest in Africa that occupies her to the present day. She was captivated with Hemingway's description of the dark continent, and she resolved to visit Africa as soon as possible. It was natural that the idea to make an African film would emerge along with the idea to visit the continent. But Riefenstahl had no desire to make another standard jungle-adventure film, nor a simple travelogue. She wanted to make a truly unique film, and to do so, she needed a new approach and an unexplored subject. That special subject came one day when Riefenstahl read an article about the slave traffic that was still flourishing from eastern Africa into greater Arabia. Sending for information from the Anti-Slavery Society in London, she learned that over 50,000 kidnapped natives were being sold into slavery each year. For Riefenstahl, it was an ideal topic. She conceived the film to be a mixture of feature film and documentary. At the same time the film was taking shape in her head, a book entitled *Schwarze Fracht* (Black Cargo) was published, dealing with the same subject. Riefenstahl bought both the film rights to the book and the use of the name. Once again, she started the difficult preparations for filmmaking: arranging financing and searching for locations.

It was during the search for locations that the first of many misfortunes occurred. Traveling one day with two assistants from Nairobi to northeastern Kenya, the Land Rover in which they were riding swerved to avoid an animal that had suddenly appeared on the road. In doing so, the Land Rover hit two stones marking the edge of a bridge over a dry river bed. The vehicle flew into the air, hurling Riefenstahl head first through the windshield. She landed unconscious in the dry river bed below, suffering a fractured skull, a damaged lung, and all her ribs broken.

It was a road that was seldom used. Luckily, a British district officer, whose job was to inspect the road once a month, happened to be making his inspection that very day and arrived at the scene less than two hours after the accident. He was able to get the victims to Gorissa, 367 miles north of Nairobi, where a small plane brought Riefenstahl to a Nairobi hospital. Riefenstahl, who at first appeared to be near death, was forced to remain in the hospital for several weeks to recover.

During her recovery in Nairobi, Riefenstahl rebounded and used the time to write the script for *Black Cargo*.

Returning to her familiar theme of a strong-willed woman in an adventurous situation, *Black Cargo* concerned a woman anthropologist's attempt to continue the work of her husband, who had died mysteriously while researching a primitive tribe in Central Africa. After a long and exciting safari, she finally finds the tribe, only to learn that they are being forced into slavery by Arab slave traders. Working with a British undercover agent, she helps to free the enslaved tribe as they are being secretly transported to Arabia. After discovering that her husband had been murdered by the slave traders, she learns from the natives of a cave with mysterious letters and pictures scratched in the wall, the long-sought key to the history of the Central African people and culture, the object of her husband's quest.

This project had particular importance for Riefenstahl: it was not only a film, it was a cause. Perhaps reacting to the charges of her earlier political indifference, Riefenstahl wrote in the preface to her treatment:

> For years, men have kept silent concerning the shameful fact that even today, in the darkest corners of the earth, men are hunted down and sold into slavery. Only through the urgent call by the Belgian missionary La Graviere to the United Nations to take care of the slave problem has it become known to the general public that the slave trade by no means belongs to the past. . . .
>
> Each month up to 5000 blacks from equatorial Africa are abducted from their homes and sold primarily to the newly-rich oil sheiks in Arabia. A strong, young man or beautiful girl costs between $1600 and $4000. . . .
>
> Despite their most strenuous efforts, the responsible authorities of the UN and the Anti-Slavery Society have been unsuccessful in putting a definite stop to the hunting and trading of slaves. The work of the police is made especially difficult by the vastness and impenetrability of the Central African bush, and the cries for help from many enslaved persons still go unheard. . . .
>
> Like the missionary La Graviere's rousing memorandum, the goal of the film *Black Cargo* is to turn the

attention of the civilized world to the problem of the
slave trade. The treatment is original, but is based upon
facts and original records.[10]

With the script in hand, the project's momentum was
regained, and preparations proceeded once again. It was not
until she started test shooting with a small team that the next
catastrophe struck. It was the autumn of 1956, and just as the
shooting began, the Suez War broke out. The bulk of the
equipment needed for the shooting and for the expedition
was on a boat that spent two months trying to get through the
Suez Canal. When it finally arrived, the rainy season had
begun. The resulting tribulations of trying to cross 2,000
kilometers of African territory to the Congo by automobile
during that difficult season quickly used all of the film's
production funds, an extraordinary expense that would have
been avoided had the equipment arrived on schedule. Once
again, it appeared that war would doom another film for Leni
Riefenstahl.

Riefenstahl hurried back to Germany to consult with an
associate who was arranging the film's financing through a
distribution company. On her arrival in Germany, she learned
that tragedy had also struck the associate and his wife. Just as
in Riefenstahl's accident, their car had swerved off a road into
a ravine in Austria, and neither was expected to survive the
accident. Although they eventually recovered, the accident
spelled the end for *Black Cargo.*

Too many misfortunes and a depleted budget prevented
Riefenstahl from filming *Black Cargo,* but it did not extinguish
the deep feeling of love that had grown within her for Africa,
nor her determination to make a film about her newly
discovered passion.

CHAPTER VIII

THE NUBA

What Leni Riefenstahl was seeking in Africa was something far more than the romanticized version presented in Hemingway's writings. She was looking for a total escape from the pressures of civilization, with its noisy and bulging cities, scandal-seeking newspapers (which had already plagued her enough), and corruption.

Her search was not new; it was the same impulse that had attracted her to the mountains as she watched her first mountain film in Berlin. They interested Riefenstahl because of their rugged, undeveloped nature. The Alps that she discovered in the 1920's were completely different from the commercialized mass tourist centers that they are today. The plush resorts had not yet been built and the autobahns had not yet penetrated the valleys. The cable cars were few, and those who wanted to behold the beauty of the Alps from a mountain summit had to reach the top on their own energy. For *The Blue Light,* Riefenstahl and her cameraman Hans Schneeberger had done all their exploring for locations on foot, meeting along the way villagers who had no idea what a motion picture was. Society had not yet forced its way into the Alps.

Today, all that has vanished, and Leni Riefenstahl is no longer attracted to the European mountains. She went to Africa searching for those untouched aspects of man and nature that she had once found not far from her home in Berlin.

During her first exposure to Africa, she was disappointed.

131

Looking fruitlessly in East Africa for natives who had remained untouched by either white or Arab intrusion, she began to despair. Some tribes had been converted to Christianity by missionaries and had given up the tribal folkways that did not agree with their adopted religion. White merchants followed and introduced money, and along with it, the accompanying vices of greed and theft that had formerly been unknown to the communal tribes. Those that had not been won to Christianity and the ways of the white Europeans had been Islamicized by the Arabs from the East. And since the Prophet Muhammed held that nudity is an offense to the eyes, the previously naked tribes had been forced to don foreign and impractical clothes. Worse yet, the tribes that had been Christianized began warring with the Islamic tribes. Riefenstahl began to fear that she had arrived too late to find the Africa she had expected.

The day before she was to return to Europe, Riefenstahl happened to be leafing through some photo magazines and was suddenly struck by a photograph that embodied everything she had been looking for. It was a photo taken by a well-known English photographer named George Rodger and was entitled "A Nuba of Kordofan." It was a picture of two Nuban wrestlers, one mounted on the shoulders of the other. Anyone acquainted with *Olympia* who then studies this remarkable photo will understand why Riefenstahl was attracted to it. The wrestlers had the same physical perfection that she had so often highlighted in *Olympia*. The composition of the photo is even similar to Riefenstahl's own composition in *Olympia,* suggesting the familiar style of "statues on film." Riefenstahl vowed that she would return to Africa and find this striking tribe.

It wasn't until 1962 that Riefenstahl returned to search for the Nubas. She joined a German scientific expedition that was exploring the Sudan and East Africa. During the course of this expedition, she finally made contact with the natives of the photograph, but only after suffering countless difficulties in securing the necessary visitation permits from the Sudanese government and then confronting the natural obstacles of traveling through uncharted land without the benefit of even the most primitive roads.

Suddenly, one day, deep into southern Sudan, Riefenstahl spotted figures darting around in the rocks high above her. Following the figures, she came upon hundreds of Nubas watching a wrestling contest. The wrestlers were straight from Rodger's photo. She had finally found the Nubas.

Riefenstahl, who was then sixty years old, left the German expedition and remained with the Nubas for six months, gradually winning their friendship and learning their language. The more she learned, the more she realized the importance of her discovery. The Nubas were a tribe that knew no theft, murder, or other human vices. They still followed their old tribal ways, untouched by the influence of either Western or Arabic civilizations. They were farmers, not nomads, and although they had to work hard to survive, they still had time for their pleasures: wrestling for the men and dancing for the women.

Riefenstahl decided once again to become a documentary filmmaker. But this time, it was out of a personal passion of her own and not because of someone else's suggestion. Lacking the resources she had had for *Triumph of the Will* and *Olympia,* this would be her purest and most personal documentary. The decision to film was also made out of a sense of urgency. Civilization was rapidly creeping in on the isolated Nubas. Riefenstahl had arrived just in time, but she realized that the qualities of their lifestyle that she admired so much would not last much longer. If they were to be recorded for history and the benefit of future anthropologists, it was up to her, and there wasn't any time to lose.

Because of financial considerations, Riefenstahl decided to film her Nuba documentary in 16mm and in the color format, since one of the most outstanding features of Nuban beauty was their ability to paint their bodies in many different colors and designs, often resembling abstract paintings. Also, the beauty of the stark land in which the Nubas lived could only be filmed effectively in color.

Since her 1962 discovery, Riefenstahl returned to the Nubas every two years, living among them for the six to seven months of the annual dry season, learning their language and way of life, and becoming accepted into the tribe. Filming progressed with the help of her assistant, Horst Kettner, a distant relative. Kettner served as cameraman, with Riefenstahl issuing precise directions. In addition, Riefenstahl occupied herself increasingly with 35mm photographing alongside Kettner's filming. To finance the cost of the expeditions she had to assemble simply to reach the Nuba with her camera equipment, Riefenstahl sold color stills to photo-news magazines such as the West German *Stern* and *The* [London] *Sunday Times*. The stills attracted the attention of *Modern Photography* magazine, which ran a feature story on her life's work but emphasized her Nuba work. In 1973, a collection of the stills was published in a book entitled *The Last of the Nuba,* with Riefenstahl writing the text.[1] The photos depict the unique folkways of the Nubas: their dances, wrestling contests, harvests, love and mating practices, burial practices, and their everyday life. Riefenstahl embarked on the road to a new fame, that of photographer as well as filmmaker.

Riefenstahl returned to the Mesakin Nuba in January, 1974, her first visit in five years. The experience was disillusioning; in the intervening years, the Mesakin had lost those qualities that she had found so appealing. The cheerful expressions had left their faces, and houses that had never known doors now had tree trunks barring entrance. Theft, previously unheard of, was now a frequent occurrence. Somehow the Mesakin had grown ashamed of their nudity, which they covered with unsightly rags. The cause and pattern of the changes differ little from those found in most developing countries. Poor harvests caused an exodus of young men from the village in search of work, and a substantial number eventually found their way to Khartoum, the capital of the Sudan. The habits and vices of urban life returned with them to the villages, proving a deadly contaminant for the Nuba life style. Unwilling to accept the death of a primitive lifestyle she had grown to cherish, Riefenstahl left the Mesakin in search of another Nuba tribe she had heard of during an earlier visit, whom she hoped still lived in the isolation previously enjoyed by the Mesakin. Striking out into unfamiliar terrain, with limited gasoline supplies and only a few days remaining before her scheduled departure from the Sudan, Riefenstahl, Kettner, and their guide stumbled upon the object of their search, a tribe of Nubas known for ritualistic knife-fighting. Although she had to leave shortly after their discovery, Riefenstahl returned for an extended stay in December, 1974.

The Nuba of Kau, inhabitants of the southeastern corner of Kordofan province of the Sudan, bear little resemblance to the Mesakin, who dwell in the southwestern corner of the same province. This new tribe was extremely suspicious and did not welcome Riefenstahl into their midst as the Mesakin Nubas had done. It was not until her assistant, Horst Kettner, had cured the illnesses of several of their children that they gradually allowed Riefenstahl to study the tribe. Unfortunately, they continued to fear her cameras and would not knowingly allow her to film them. Most of the filming of the Kau Nuba she did on the sly, often while hiding behind rocks with telephoto lenses. Riefenstahl used stills from this visit for a second book on the Nuba, *People of Kau*.[2] The photos portray the intense beauty of the Kau Nubas, with statuesque physiques not unlike those of Olympic champions. Her fascination with the human body, so obvious throughout all of her work, extends to her still photography of the Nuba tribes. The expedition's greatest success came when she was able to surreptitiously film one of the strangest practices of the Kau, "the dance of the knives." In this competition, two of the tribe's strongest warriors tie razor-sharp blades to their arms and legs and slash each other until one collapses through loss of blood.

While living with primitive tribes might seem strenuous enough for most people in their seventies, Riefenstahl, at the age of seventy-two, lied about her age by twenty years to enroll in a scuba-diving class at an Indian Ocean resort hotel. With the same single-minded pursuit exhibited in her youthful obsession with alpine sports, she embarked on a series of diving trips to the Caribbean, the Red Sea, and the Maldive Islands, eventually adding underwater filming and photography to her diving exercises. Again, with the assistance of Horst Kettner, she began work on a new film, now dealing with the ocean depths rather than the mountain heights. In 1978, she published a collection of her underwater photos under the title *Coral Gardens*.[3]

Despite her frenetic lifestyle, age eventually caught up with Leni Riefenstahl. She suffered broken bones from a skiing accident in St. Moritz, eventually requiring several operations. Bad investments, including one disastrous misplaced confidence that virtually wiped out her life savings, took their toll on her outlook on life. Eventually, she recognized the need to ration her dwindling energies and make priorities in her ongoing projects. All her life she had talked of writing her memoirs; indeed, her meticulous personal archives existed for that purpose. Several fruitless efforts to engage a suitable ghostwriter convinced Riefenstahl that the effort must be her own. *Leni Riefenstahl Memoiren*[4] finally saw publication in Germany in 1987. Footage from her Nuba and underwater expeditions remain, unedited, in the editing room of her house in suburban Munich.[5]

CHAPTER IX

LEGAL RIGHTS

Adequate protection of artistic and intellectual property poses a major challenge even under normal circumstances. When a nation's institutions collapse and cease to exist as they did with the fall of Nazi Germany in 1945, efforts to establish or reclaim legal rights often take on Kafkaesque dimensions. Studio giants such as *Ufa* disappeared, along with many of the financing institutions. The Nazi Party and the Film Division of the Propaganda Ministry, both major film producers, likewise vanished in the ashes of the Third Reich. Eventually Murnau Stiftung and Transit Film were established in West Germany to act as repositories of rights for films produced by the Nazi Party, the government, or corporations no longer extant. In this legal maze Riefenstahl continually attempted to assert legal and financial claims to her films.

Both a blessing and a curse throughout her career, *Triumph of the Will* also offers the most commercial rewards, a fact not lost on Riefenstahl. Arguably one of the world's most pirated films, the use of footage from *Triumph of the Will* in film and television documentaries is commonplace. While she argues that most of her efforts have concentrated on preventing others from illegally profiting from the film, the climate of most of the postwar years certainly restricted her own ability to realize its financial potential. When Erwin Leiser's 1961 film production, *Mein Kampf,* became an international success, however, Riefenstahl made her move. Incensed that a substantial portion of the film consisted of footage from *Triumph of the Will* (according to Riefenstahl, nearly 600 meters of film[1]) obtained without permission from either herself or Transit-Film, she brought suit in the West German courts. The courts denied Riefenstahl's claims to the film, finding that the Nazi Party, and not Riefenstahl's film production company, had produced the film. According to Riefenstahl, the courts relied heavily on Ufa advertising that stressed the party's role in the film production, while denying as evidence affidavits introduced by Riefenstahl's attorneys. The affidavits lacked the necessary official notarization for legal submission as evidence; the disallowal was not known until after the decision.[2] Riefenstahl maintains that Ufa used the film as an opportunity to enhance the company's relations with the Nazi Party, hence the heavy advertising campaign linking the film with the party. Following her judicial loss, she reluctantly approached an old-time personal enemy, Arnold Raether, to substantiate her position. As the head of the Nazi Party's Film Division, Raether vigorously opposed Hitler's selection of Riefenstahl as director of the first Party Rally film, *Sieg des Glaubens,* which Riefenstahl readily admits was a party production. Their personal animosity grew, and Riefenstahl maintains it was one of the main reasons Hitler agreed to *Triumph of the Will* being a production of Leni Riefenstahl Film rather than the Nazi Party Film Division. To Riefenstahl's surprise, Raether agreed to overlook old animosities and executed a notarized affidavit declaring that *Triumph of the Will* was a production of Leni Riefenstahl Productions, that Riefenstahl had assumed all aspects of production, including financing, and that the Nazi Party was not involved. He further stated that the orders for non-involvement came directly from Hitler, as a result of difficulties arising from the first party film production at Nuremberg, *Sieg des Glaubens.* The West German court decision stands, regardless of Raether's declarations. Riefenstahl did not appeal the decision.

The commercial potential for *Triumph of the Will,* in any case, exists in the United States, not in West Germany. Under West German law, publication of *Mein Kampf* remains illegal, even for historical reasons. Restrictions exist for the showing of films with Hitler in them; portraits of Hitler are against the law. The American fascination with the Hitler period, however, created a booming black market in dupes of *Triumph of the Will,* dupes copied so many times that the washout of blacks and whites severely damaged film quality. Riefenstahl decided on action in the United States.

Legal rights to her films proved to be as complicated in the United States as they were in West Germany. The copyright office at the Library of Congress informed Riefenstahl that Raymond Rohauer, a film collector, distributor, and exhibitor of decidedly mixed reputation, had registered the copyrights for both Olympic films. In her memoirs, Riefenstahl describes a visit with Rohauer, who was accompanied, interestingly enough, by Buster Keaton. Riefenstahl does not admit to a legal arrangement with Rohauer as a result of that meeting, but she does complain that although he promised her fifty percent of his profits from her films, he never delivered "a single mark."[3]

According to advice from officials at the Library of Congress, her only alternative to lengthy legal processes was to make small changes in the films, such as the addition of English subtitles, and then to submit prints to the Library of Congress, establishing copyrights on the new prints. Riefenstahl commenced the costly and time-consuming task of changing films and striking new prints, and in 1975, registered new copyrights for *The Blue Light, Triumph of the Will, Olympia* (parts 1 and 2), and *Tiefland.* Abiding by the old real-estate axiom that "possession is nine-tenths of ownership," Riefenstahl reasoned that her possession of the original negatives of the films, allowing her nearly perfect print reproduction, constituted a greater competitive advantage in the marketplace than the constant threat of legal action against film pirates. Since securing her 1975 copyrights, Riefenstahl contracted with Janus Films of New York for the American rights, using prints from her negatives. All but *The Blue Light* and *Tiefland* are now available on videocassette.

NOTES

Chapter I

1. *Der Heilige Berg* (The Holy Mountain), 1926; *Der Grosse Sprung* (The Great Leap), 1927; *Das Weisse Stadion* (The White Stadium), 1928; *Die Weisse Hölle vom Piz Palü* (The White Hell of Piz Palü), 1929; *Stürme über dem Montblanc* (Storm over the Montblanc), 1930; *Der Weisse Rausch* (The White Frenzy), 1931; *S.O.S. Eisberg* (S.O.S. Iceberg), 1933; and *Der Ewige Traum* (The Eternal Dream), 1934.
2. Leni Riefenstahl, *Kampf in Schnee und Eis* (Leipzig: Hesse und Becker Verlag, 1933), pp. 10–15. Translation by the author.
3. Roland Schacht was the brother of Hjalmar Schacht, who became the Nazi minister of finance.
4. *Close up,* Territet, Switzerland, December 1929.
5. A perfunctory sound version of *The White Hell of Piz Palü* was released in 1935, and is generally the version seen today.
6. Dr. Arnold Fanck, *Regie mit Gletschern, Stürmen, und Lawinen* (Munich: Nymphenburger Verlagshandlung, 1973), p. 146. Translation by the author.
7. L. Andrew Mannheim, "Leni," *Modern Photography* (February 1974), p. 113.
8. "Filmografie," *Filmkritik* (August 1972), pp. 436–437.
9. Mannheim, *op. cit.,* p. 117.
10. *Berliner Morgenpost,* Berlin, April 1932.
11. Trude Weiss, "The Blue Light," *Close Up* (June 1932), pp. 119–123.
12. Siegfried Kracauer, *From Caligari to Hitler* (Princeton, NJ: Princeton University Press), p. 112.
13. Susan Sontag, "Fascinating Fascism," *The New York Review of Books* (February 6, 1975), p. 26.
14. Fanck, *op. cit.,* p. 165.

15. Peter Wollen, *Signs and Meaning in the Cinema* (Bloomington, IN: Indiana University Press, 1969), p. 94.
16. "Filmografie," *op. cit.,* p. 437.

Chapter II

1. Fritz Hanfstängl, *Hitler—The Missing Years* (London, 1956).
2. *The Blue Light* was scored by Giuseppe Becce, and *Day of Freedom* by the famous German film composer Peter Kreuder.
3. Herman Weigel, "Interview mit Leni Riefenstahl," *Filmkritik* (August 1972), p. 396.
4. Only three German feature films dealt directly with Nazi Party history, and all three were made in 1933, the Nazi's first year of power. They were *S. A. Mann Brandt, Hitlerjunge Quex,* and *Hans Westmar.*
5. Herman Weigel, "Randbemerkungen zum Thema," *Filmkritik* (August 1972), pp. 427–428.
6. *Ibid.,* p. 428.
7. Remarks made by Leni Riefenstahl during an interview with the author, August, 1975.
8. Robert Gardner, "Can the Will Triumph?" *Film Comment* (Winter 1965), p. 29.
9. Museum of Modern Art film print, *Triumph of the Will.* All references to the film itself refer to this complete print. For information on how this print was preserved through the war, see comments by Eileen Bowser, Museum of Modern Art Curatorial Assistant, in "Leni Riefenstahl and the Museum of Modern Art," *Film Comment* (Winter 1965), p. 16.
10. The S.A., or "Sturmabteilung," were the so-called "Brown-shirts" of the Nazi Party. Besides being responsible for maintaining order at party meetings, they were the Nazi's street brawlers against rival political parties. They were in organization and purpose different from the S.S., or "Black-shirts."
11. Hamilton T. Burden, *The Nuremberg Party Rallies: 1923–39* (New York: Frederick A. Praeger, 1967), p. 77.
12. William L. Shirer, *Berlin Diary* (New York: Popular Library, 1940), pp. 20–21.
13. Michel Delahaye, "Leni and the Wolf: Interview with Leni Riefenstahl," *Cahiers du Cinema in English* (No. 5), p. 54.
14. Ken Kelman, "Propaganda as Vision—Triumph of the Will," *Film Culture* (Spring 1973), p. 163.

15. Burden, *op. cit.*
16. The dates for the "City Awakening" sequence cannot be determined, but since they record no significant events, dates are not important. The remarks made by the various speakers in Sequence V, "Opening of the Party Congress," were made on many different occasions and locations, and edited together for this sequence.
17. Delahaye, *op. cit.*, pp. 51–52.
18. *Ibid.*, p. 54.
19. Siegfried Kracauer, *From Caligari to Hitler: A Psychological History of the German Film* (Princeton, New Jersey: Princeton University Press, 1947), illustrations 59–60.
20. *Ibid.*, p. 290.
21. To obtain these shots, Riefenstahl had to make a personal appeal to Hitler for permission to have a cameraman ride with him in the automobile during the parade. (Comments by Riefenstahl to the author.)
22. Kevin Brownlow, "Leni Riefenstahl," *Film* (Winter 1966), p. 18.
23. Albert Speer, *Inside the Third Reich* (New York: The Macmillan Company, 1970), p. 62.
24. Remarks made by Leni Riefenstahl during an interview with the author, August, 1975.
25. David Stewart Hull, *Film in the Third Reich* (Berkeley and Los Angeles: University of California Press, 1969), p. 75.
26. Speer, *op. cit.*, pp. 58–59.
27. Roger Manvell and Heinrich Fraenkel, *The German Cinema* (New York: Praeger Publishers, 1971), p. 78.
28. Leni Riefenstahl, *Hinter den Kulissen des Reichsparteitag Films* (Munich: Franz Eher Verlag, 1935), p. 9.
29. Kracauer, *op. cit.*, p. 301.
30. Riefenstahl, *op. cit.*, p. 20.
31. *Ibid.*, p. 24.
32. Correspondence between Emil Schünemann and the Reichsfachschaftfilm e.V., (Berlin Document Center, Berlin).
33. Riefenstahl has denied in an interview (Herman Weigel, "Interview mit Leni Riefenstahl," *Filmkritik,* August 1972, p. 400) that she wrote the book, and says that it was written by Ernst Jäger. Her claim is substantiated by a receipt for Reichsmarks 1000 written by Jäger to Riefenstahl for the writing of the book, which can be found in the Bundesarchiv in Koblenz. Further, the former publicity director of Ufa has sworn in an affidavit that Jäger was the author.

34. Richard Corliss, "Leni Riefenstahl: A Bibliography," *Film Heritage* (Fall 1969), p. 30.

Chapter III

1. Ernst Jäger was the ghostwriter of the book on the making of *Triumph of the Will* which bears Riefenstahl's name as author (*Hinter den Kulissens des Reichsparteitag Films*).
2. "Interview with Henry Jaworsky," *Film Culture* (Spring 1973), p. 123.
3. *Ibid.*
4. Michel Delahaye, "Leni and the Wolf: Interview with Leni Riefenstahl," *Cahiers du Cinema in English,* No. 5, pp. 52–53.
5. Riefenstahl employs the same system today with her personal archives, which she has meticulously kept since her early days as a dancer. An entire wall of her living room is full of binders, color-coded according to stills, letters, and documents, with each binder subject-indexed within the color code.
6. L. Andrew Mannheim, "Leni," *Modern Photography* (February 1974), p. 116.
7. *Ibid.,* p. 117.
8. According to Riefenstahl, her copy of this letter was lost when the French confiscated her possessions at the end of the war.
9. Budd Schulberg, "Nazi Pin-Up Girl," *The Saturday Evening Post* (March 30, 1946).
10. Henry McLemore, "Propaganda? Not in this Film!" Hollywood Citizen News, December 16, 1938.
11. Editorial, *Los Angeles Times,* December 17, 1938.
12. Susan Sontag, "Leni Riefenstahl and Fascism," *The New York Review of Books* (February 6, 1975), p. 26.
13. Richard Corliss, "Leni Riefenstahl: A Bibliography," *Film Heritage* (Fall 1969), p. 32.

Chapter IV

1. The obituary for the opera's composer, Eugen d'Albert, appearing in the *Berliner Morgenpost* on March 4, 1932, noted that "There is scarcely an opera fan today who doesn't know d'Albert's *Tiefland.*"

2. *Der Grosse König* was made in 1942 by the director of *Jud Süss,* Veit Harlan, on the personal orders of Dr. Goebbels.
3. In an interview with the author, Speer commented on Riefenstahl's request: "It was wartime. It couldn't be done. As a minister, I had no other choice. I had to make the decision that I did."

Chapter V

1. *Der Film—Die Illustrierte Wochenschrift* (May 18, 1940), 1 Beilage zu Nummer 20.
2. Harald Reinl has been commercially successful in the postwar German film industry, making largely action-adventure films aimed at youthful audiences. In 1967 he filmed a remake of Fritz Lang's *Die Nibelungen.*
3. Speer's grandiose plans are well described, with excellent illustrations, in his memoirs, *Inside the Third Reich.*
4. This letter can be found at the American Document Center in Berlin.
5. The fact that he had become creatively exhausted and forced to depend on Riefenstahl for employment during the war seems to have deeply damaged Fanck's ego. In the 395 pages of his 1973 memoirs, Fanck devotes one short paragraph to his wartime filmmaking, without ever mentioning the fact that he was employed by Leni Riefenstahl. His attitude towards Riefenstahl after the war and until his death seems to be one of increasing jealousy, and, seemingly, hatred. While his memoirs boast of how he discovered Riefenstahl, succeeding mentions of her name are devoted to discrediting her personally. When advertisements for a television showing of *SOS Eisberg* in 1973 advertised the film as starring Leni Riefenstahl and Ernst Udet, while making no mention of Fanck as director, he wrote indignant letters of protest. But by that time, no one listened.
6. Information supplied by Walter Traut in correspondence with the author, December 16, 1975.
7. Dr. Arnold Fanck, *Regie mit Gletschern, Stürmen, und Lawinen* (Munich: Nymphenburger Verlagshandlung, 1973), p. 376.
8. When Berlin was occupied, Breker's studio was emptied by American troops and the uncompleted work thrown into rubbish heaps outside. The destruction of the official art work of the defeated Nazi regime was so complete that thirty years later, when the Frankfurt Art Museum attempted to stage an

exhibit of Nazi art in connection with observances of the thirtieth anniversary of Nazi Germany's defeat, none of the major statues by Thorak or Breker still existed. They were represented in the exhibit only through photographic blow-ups.

Chapter VI

1. Leni Riefenstahl, "Why I am Filming Penthesilea," *Film Culture* (Spring 1973), p. 194.
2. *Ibid.,* p. 195.
3. *Ibid.,* p. 197.
4. *Ibid.,* p. 199.
5. *Ibid.,* p. 202.
6. *Ibid.,* p. 201.
7. *Ibid.*
8. *Ibid.,* p. 209.
9. *Ibid.,* pp. 213–215.

Chapter VII

1. During World War I, Dr. Fanck worked for the German espionage corps, specializing in microfilm techniques, then a new art for professional spies. He was once flown to Holland to microfilm a book of British naval codes that "Mademoiselle Docteur" had stolen for an evening, and which she had to return the next morning before it was discovered missing. This incident is related in Fanck's memoirs.
2. Herman Weigel, "Interview mit Leni Riefenstahl," *Filmkritik* (August 1972), p. 399.
3. "Filmografie," *Filmkritik* (August 1972), p. 224.
4. The 1952 film *House of Wax,* filmed in 3-D, had generated long lines at the box office and, at the time of the planning of *The Red Devils,* interest in this new process either as a gimmick or as a potential contribution to the art form was still high.
5. The completed shooting script for *The Red Devils* is in Leni Riefenstahl's personal archives.
6. Leni Riefenstahl, "Treatment for *The Red Devils:* a Comedy in the Snow" (copyrighted and unpublished film treatment by Leni Riefenstahl, made available to the author).

7. *Ibid.*
8. *Ibid.*
9. *Ibid.*
10. *Ibid.*

Chapter VIII

1. Leni Riefenstahl, *The Last of the Nuba* (New York: Harper & Row), 1973.
2. Leni Riefenstahl, *People of Kau* (New York: Harper & Row), 1976.
3. Leni Riefenstahl, *Coral Gardens* (New York: Harper & Row), 1978.
4. Leni Riefenstahl, *Leni Riefenstahl Memoiren* (Munich: Albrecht Knaus Verlag), 1987.
5. *Ibid.,* p. 903.

Chapter IX

1. Leni Riefenstahl, *Leni Riefenstahl Memoiren* (Munich: Albrecht Knaus Verlag, 1987), p. 767.
2. *Ibid.,* pp. 767–768.
3. *Ibid.,* p. 848.

APPENDIX A

PRIZES AWARDED TO RIEFENSTAHL

Silver Medaille at the 1932 Bienniale in Venice for *The Blue Light.*

German Film Prize in 1935 for *Triumph of the Will.*

International Grand Prix for *Triumph of the Will* at the 1937 Paris World Exhibition.

Grand Prize for *Triumph of the Will* at Venice Film Festival in 1935.

German Film Prize for *Olympia* in 1938.

Grand Prize for *Olympia* at Venice Film Festival in 1938.

Diploma for the Olympic Gold Medal for *Olympia* from the International Olympics Committee. (Riefenstahl was awarded the Gold Medal in 1939, but because of the war, she never received the medal. In 1948, she received a diploma certifying the award of the Gold Medal but did not receive the medal itself.

Awards for *Olympia* conferred by the governments of Greece and Sweden.

APPENDIX B

TIEFLAND: THE OPERA AND THE FILM

by Herbert Windt, Music Composer for the Film

One must consider the total music of d'Albert's opera *Tiefland* before it can be compared to the film of the same name. When examined closely, the differences become apparent. If the question concerned merely a filming of the opera (with the singers and everything else), there would be no problem. But the moment the singers stop singing and begin to talk and act like normal people, an artistic split is caused: the music of the opera no longer fits its new context. Why? Because every opera is stylized; if it were not, it wouldn't be an opera. The film, on the other hand, is derived from reality, from the real world. That is the distinguishing characteristic. There are other things to take into consideration: the opera *Tiefland* belongs to the class of so-called *Veristischen* operas which have developed from the naturalist movement. On the other side is Leni Riefenstahl's *Tiefland* film, which even though it is closely connected to naturalism, is still in a form that can only be referred to as "stylized."

But since all music is stylized, isn't it paradoxical that the two don't fit together? The reason is that the pathos of the naturalist opera is on a totally different level from the pathos of the stylized film. Therefore, the task for me was to determine what parts of the opera's music would be applicable to the film in the same artistic sense. All the singing that dominated the stage with such great intensity would be ruinous for the film. The compromise required to make the film consistent with the opera lies on a completely different level. That which we designate as *Naturmusik* in the opera is precisely that which gives a musical life to the *Tiefland* film. That means in particular the beautiful opening with the mountain motifs (where the famous clarinet solo becomes the leitmotif for Pedro); Pedro's descent into the lowlands; the wedding procession to the church; and, of course, the ending. For these sequences I could use whole sections from the original score in the conscious endeavor to use as much as possible from the original music. These musical pieces that carry the film for such long stretches of time are excellent examples to invalidate the customary musical accompaniment desired by most directors. In addition, I was able to use for shorter passages some of the opera's most beautiful motifs: some completely from the original, others in my own adaptation.

Because a large portion of the film's theme is completely different from the plot of the opera, it was often necessary to compose completely new music. This new music, even though distinctly different from d'Albert's, nevertheless successfully counterpointed his music. I tried to unite the two, incorporating the themes of d'Albert into my music. The music also incorporated original Spanish dances and melodies, which I borrowed from the rich heritage of Spanish folk music.

I hope that my work has been a contribution to the work as a whole, and I think that the success of the film will be a reflection on all who helped to create it. And above all, it will be a reflection of its creator, Leni Riefenstahl, who has a "sixth sense" about what is right in musical matters!

Unpublished essay by
Herbert Windt dated
December 17, 1953
(Translation by the
author)

APPENDIX C

DECISION OF THE BADEN STATE COMMISSION FOR CLEANSING, DECISION CHAMBER FREIBURG

Leni Riefenstahl, film actress, film director, and business manager living in Königsfeld in the Black Forest, was born on August 22, 1902, in Berlin and is divorced and childless. She was neither a member of the Nazi Party nor any of its divisions, organizations, or unions. The Judgment Chamber, Department 2, Freiburg, at its session of 6 July 1949, has designated the above named as "not in violation of the law."

It is formally established that Frau Leni Riefenstahl was not a member of the Nazi Party nor any of its divisions; consequently, there is no suspicion of guilt under Directive 38. However, it remains to be examined, if and to what extent Frau Riefenstahl promoted the National Socialist tyranny in other ways through her cooperation with the party or its divisions; or, if she emerges as a beneficiary of the same. For this part of the examination, the accused must not be presumed guilty, but on the contrary, full proof of guilt must be established.

The investigation into the relationships of Frau Riefenstahl with leading personalities of the "Third Reich" proves that, contrary to the many widespread rumors and assertions made by the public and in the press, no relationships were established that went beyond what was necessary for the execution of her artistic undertakings. In particular, no proof could be found to justify the claim that a close personal, or even intimate, relationship with Hitler existed. The com-

pleted investigations of the American and French occupation authorities have produced the same results. There was not a single witness or piece of evidence to prove that a close relationship existed between Hitler and Riefenstahl. Furthermore, this conclusion is supported by numerous sworn affidavits, several of which are from Hitler's immediate circle. The interrogation of Frau Riefenstahl conducted by the chamber did not shake the chamber's conviction, but rather, strengthened it. Frau Riefenstahl proved herself to be a thoroughly honest and believable witness, and even where her own statements could have been unfavorable to her, she did not hold back or try to vacillate in her responses. The furnished photocopies of the two telegrams change nothing.*
One of the telegrams does not appear on an official telegram form and therefore lacks any proof of its authenticity; it has been dismissed by Frau Riefenstahl as "a clumsy fake." As for the second telegram, Frau Riefenstahl's whereabouts at the time of its sending cannot be pinpointed and the possibility of a forgery also exists.

Even if the telegrams were proven to be original, their strident and bombastic tone would indicate that a close relationship with Hitler did not exist, but rather that an attempt was being made to establish one.

Frau Riefenstahl never strove to, nor did she exercise any influence upon the political decisions of the rulers of the "Third Reich." She had absolutely nothing to do with politics either before or after the Nazi takeover of power but rather was completely involved in her artistic concerns. To produce propaganda for the Nazi Party was far removed from her thoughts. Accepting the film commissions for the party rally and Olympic films does not persuade one to the contrary. The Olympic film was an international concern and therefore

---

*The telegrams referred to here appear to be references to two telegrams that are now in the files of the Berlin Document Center. The one that does not appear on an official telegram form thanks Hitler for "providing Germany with its greatest victory, the march of German troops into Paris." The second telegram thanks Hitler for the red roses he sent to her on her birthday.

eliminates itself as an incriminating work; furthermore, the acceptance and execution of the two commissions do not by themselves constitute making propaganda for the National Socialists. In addition, Frau Riefenstahl at first emphatically refused to accept the commissions and undertook them only upon the repeated and irrevocable instructions of Hitler; therefore she lacked the clear intentions of consciously producing propaganda for the Nazis. Her efforts were aimed at producing a documentary film rather than political propaganda. After the film was critically received as a very important piece of film art, it is not the fault of the creator that the Nazis decided to exploit it for propaganda purposes at home and abroad. None of the presumptions necessary for a *dolus eventualis* can be accepted. The prizes earned by the film and its rating by international juries and press reports show that the film was not regarded abroad as propaganda. The extreme hate with which Riefenstahl was pursued by Goebbels and members of the Propaganda Ministry is proof of the fact that she was never recognized as a propagandist for the "Third Reich" by the regular party circles. Frau Riefenstahl never agreed to make propaganda or agitation films such as *Jud Süss,* even though such offers had been made to her (the Horst Wessel film and the Grossmacht-Presse film). In this connection, it must also be pointed out that at the time of the filming of the Party Rally film, the anti-Semitic Nuremberg laws had not yet been passed and the Jewish pogroms had not yet taken place. Also, the war preparations of Hitler were not yet known by outsiders, and the true nature of the movement was still disguised. For that reason, a guilty sentence on the promotion of the Nazi tyranny cannot be reached. It contradicts the facts to say that Frau Riefenstahl was an "indisputable propagandist for the National Socialists." She had, moreover, maintained friendships to the last moment with Jews, and during the Nazi regime had employed non-Aryans in her film work and had protected them from Nazi persecution. The "Heil Hitler" greeting was not customary in her circle.

With regard to the benefits that Frau Riefenstahl may have received, it suffices to point out that Frau Riefenstahl was an internationally recognized film personality even before the Nazis' assumption of power. Her main income was drawn from her earlier films and she did not apply for commissions through the party or the Nazi government; rather, she undertook the commissions only under pressure, and therefore in no way wrangled improper benefits for herself. Moreover, the contention that units of the army or inmates of concentration camps were placed at the artist's disposal for her own private business purposes is proven false. Army units were never marched in front of her so that she could choose a suitable actor for *Tiefland,* and the gypsies that did act in that film were voluntarily recruited and did not come from concentration camps.

To examine to what extent her competitors in the film industry were involved in the propagation of misleading rumors about Frau Riefenstahl is not the business of the court; the task of the court was only to examine the veracity of the rumors, and the court's findings were negative. In order that no formal nor material incriminations against Frau Riefenstahl shall emerge, the court with a majority vote hereby declares Frau Riefenstahl to be "not in violation of the law."

APPENDIX D

FILMOGRAPHY

1926

DER HEILIGE BERG (THE HOLY MOUNTAIN)
Production company: UFA
Director: Dr. Arnold Fanck
Script: Dr. Arnold Fanck
Camera: Sepp Allgeier, Albert Benitz, Helmar Lerski, Kurt Neubert, Hans Schneeberger
Music: Edmund Reisch
Cast: Leni Riefenstahl, Luis Trenker, Friedach Richard, Friedrich Schneider, Hannes Schneider
Length: 3100 m.
Premiere: December 15, 1926

1927

DER GROSSE SPRUNG (THE GREAT LEAP)
Production company: UFA
Director: Dr. Arnold Fanck
Script: Dr. Arnold Fanck
Camera: Sepp Allgeier, Richard Angst, Albert Benitz, Charles Metain, Kurt Neubert, Hans Schneeberger
Music: Werner Heymann
Cast: Leni Riefenstahl, Luis Trenker, Hans Schneeberger, Paul Graetz
Length: 2931 m.
Premiere: December 20, 1927

1929

DAS SCHICKSAL DERER VON HAPSBURG (THE DESTINY
OF THE HOUSE OF HAPSBURG)
Production companies: Leofilm, Essemfilm
Director: Rudolf Raffè
Script: Max Ferner
Camera: Marius Holdt
Cast: Erna Morena, Fritz Spira, Leni Riefenstahl, Maly Debschaft,
Alfons Fryland, Franz Kammauf
Length: approximately 2400 m.
Premiere: early 1929

DIE WEISSE HÖLLE VON PIZ PALÜ (THE WHITE HELL OF
PIZ PALÜ)
Production company: H. R. Sokal-Film GmbH
Script: Dr. Arnold Fanck, Ladislaus Vajda (after an idea by Fanck)
Camera: Sepp Allgeier, Richard Angst, Hans Schneeberger
Cast: Leni Riefenstahl, Gustav Diessl, Ernst Petersen, Ernst Udet,
Mizzi Gotzel, Otto Spring
Length: 3210 m.
Premiere: November 15, 1929

1930

STÜRME ÜBER DEM MONTBLANC (STORM OVER MONT
BLANC)
Production company: Aafa-Film AG
Director: Dr. Arnold Fanck
Script: Dr. Arnold Fanck
Camera: Sepp Allgeier, Richard Angst, Hans Schneeberger
Music: Paul Dessau
Cast: Leni Riefenstahl, Sepp Rist, Ernst Udet, Mathias Wieman,
Friedrich Kayssler, and others
Length: 2964 m.
Premiere: December 25, 1930

1932–33

DAS BLAUE LICHT (THE BLUE LIGHT)
Production company: Leni Riefenstahl-Film

Producer: Walter Traut
Director: Leni Riefenstahl
Script: Leni Riefenstahl, Bela Balazs (from a legend of the Dolomites heard by Leni Riefenstahl)
Camera: Hans Schneeberger
Music: Giuseppe Becce
Cast: Leni Riefenstahl, Mathias Wieman, Max Holzboer, Beni Fuhrer, Martha Mair, Franz Maldacea, and villagers of Sarentino
Length: 2344 m.
Premiere: March 24, 1932

SOS EISBERG (S.O.S. ICEBERG)
Production companies: in Germany, Deutsche Universal AG; in the United States, Universal Film
Director: Dr. Arnold Fanck for the German version, Tay Garnett for the American
Script: Dr. Arnold Fanck, Fritz Loewe, Ernst Sorge, Hans Hinrich, E. Knopf, F. Wolf, Tom Reed
Camera: Richard Angst, Hans Schneeberger, Ernst Udet, Franz Schrieck (for aerial shots)
Music: Paul Dessau
Cast: Leni Riefenstahl, Ernst Udet, Gustav Diessl, Max Holzboer, and others
Length: 2827 m. (German version)
Premiere: August 30, 1933

MADEMOISELLE DOCTEUR (MADAM DOCTOR)—unrealized film
Production company: UFA
Director: G. W. Pabst
Script: Gerhard Menzel
Camera: Hans Schneeberger
Cast: Leni Riefenstahl and others
Shortly after the start of production, UFA received orders from the German government to stop production for reasons of national security. Pabst made the film in 1936 in France and without Leni Riefenstahl.

SIEG DES GLAUBENS (VICTORY OF FAITH)
Production company: Filmabteilung der NSDAP (film division of the National Socialist German Workers Party—"Nazi" Party)
Producer: Arnold Raether
Director: Leni Riefenstahl

Camera: Sepp Allgeier, Franz Weimayr, Walter Frentz
Music: Herbert Windt
Length: approximately 1700 meters
Premiere: December 1, 1933
Previous filmographies list the film division of the Propaganda
Ministry as the film's production company. In Riefenstahl's
memoirs, she cites an affidavit signed by the film's producer
Arnold Raether that the film, unlike the privately financed (by
Riefenstahl's company) *Triumph of the Will,* was produced by the
party. Raether served as head of the Nazi Party film division,
later as head of the film office of the Propaganda Ministry.
According to Riefenstahl's memoirs, Raether's personal animosity to Riefenstahl during the filming of *Sieg des Glaubens* was so
intense it caused Hitler to agree to Riefenstahl's independent
production of *Triumph of the Will.* Filmed at the 1933 Nazi party
rally in Nuremberg.

1934

TIEFLAND (THE LOWLANDS)—unrealized film project
Production companies: Leni Riefenstahl Film, Terra Film
Director: Alfred Abel (engaged when negotiations for G. W. Pabst
fell through)
Camera: Hans Schneeberger
Music: Giuseppe Becce
Cast: Leni Riefenstahl, Heinrich George, Sepp Rist
Production plans fell apart in the spring of 1934 due to scheduling
difficulties with the famous actor Heinrich George and financial
disputes with Terra Film.

1935

TRIUMPH DES WILLENS (TRIUMPH OF THE WILL)
Production company: Reichsparteitagsfilm der Leni Riefenstahl
Film (Party rally film division of Leni Riefenstahl film company)
Producer: Walter Traut
Director: Leni Riefenstahl
Camera director: Sepp Allgeier
Camera: Sepp Allgeier, Karl Altenberger, Werner Buhne, Walter
Frentz, Hans Gottschalk, Werner Hundhausen, Herbert Kebel-

mann, Albert Kling, Franz Koch, Herbert Kutschbach, Paul
Lieberenz, Richard Nickel, Walter Riml, Arthur von Schwertfeger,
Karl Vass, Franz Weimayr, Siegfried Weinmann, Karl Wellet
Production assistants: Erna Peters, Guzzi and Otto Lantschner,
Walter Prager, Wolfgang Bruning
Length: 3109 m.
Premiere: March 28, 1935
Filmed at the 1934 Nazi party rally in Nuremberg.

TAG DER FREIHEIT—UNSERE WEHRMACHT (DAY OF
FREEDOM—OUR ARMY)
Production company: Reichsparteitagsfilm der Leni Riefenstahl Film
Director: Leni Riefenstahl
Camera: Willi Zielke, Guzzi Lantschner, and four others
Length: approximately 800 m.
Premiere: December, 1935
Filmed at the 1935 Nazi party rally in Nuremberg. Like the other
two party rally films, the film title comes from the name given by
the Nazi to each party rally.

1938

OLYMPIA
Part One: FEST DER VOLKER (FESTIVAL OF THE PEOPLE)
Part Two: FEST DER SCHONHEIT (FESTIVAL OF BEAUTY)
Production company: Olympia-Film GmbH
Producer: Walter Traut
Director: Leni Riefenstahl
Music: Herbert Windt and Walter Gronostay
Camera: Hans Ertl, Walter Frentz, Guzzi Lantschner, Kurt Neu-
bert, Hans Scheib, Willi Zielke, Andor von Barsy, Wilf. Basse,
Jos. Dietze, E. Epkens, F. von Friedl, Hans Gottschalk, Richard
Groschapp, W. Hameister, Walf Hart, Hasso Hartnagel, Walter
Hege, E. von der Heyden, Albert Höcht, Paul Holzki, Werner
Hundhausen, Heinz von Jaworski, H. von Kaweczynski, H.
Kebelmann, S. Ketterer, Leo de Laforgue, Lagorio, E. Lam-
bertini, Otto Lantschner, Waldemar Lemke, Georg Lemki, C. A.
Linke, E. Nitzschemann, Albert Schattman, Wilhelm Schmidt,
Hugo Schulze, L. Schwedler, Alfred Siegert, W. Siehm, Ernst
Sorge, H. von Stwolinski, Karl Vass
Length: Part one, 3269 m.; Part two, 2712 m.
Premiere; April 20, 1938

1939

PENTHESILEA—unrealized film
Production company: Leni Riefenstahl Film
Director: Leni Riefenstahl, Jurgen Fehling (for the scenes in which
   Riefenstahl would act)
Script: Leni Riefenstahl, after the play by Heinrich von Kleist
Camera: Hans Schneeberger, Alfred Benitz
Cast: Leni Riefenstahl and others

1943

VAN GOGH—unrealized film
Conceived during a lull in the wartime filming of *Tiefland, Van
Gogh* dealt with the theme of "how a genius expresses himself."
Riefenstahl intended to shoot the dramatic scenes in black and
white and the scenes dealing with bringing a painting to life in
color. The project did not develop beyond the treatment stage.

1952

DIE HEXE VON SANTA MARIA (THE WITCH OF SANTA
   MARIA)
Renewed interest in *The Blue Light* caused Riefenstahl to recut the
   film, add a new soundtrack and contemporary framing story, and
   reissue under the title *Die Hexe von Santa Maria.*
Length: 1967 m.

1954

TIEFLAND (THE LOWLANDS)
Production company: Leni Riefenstahl-Film GmbH
Director: Leni Riefenstahl
Script: Leni Riefenstahl, Harald Reinl after the opera by Eugen
   d'Albert
Music: Herbert Windt, inspired by the music of the opera
Camera: Albert Benitz
Cast: Leni Riefenstahl, Franz Eichberger, Bernhard Minetti, Ari-

bert Wäscher, Maria Koppenhöfer, Luis Rainer, Frieda Richard, Karl Skramps, Max Holzboer
Length: 2695 m.
Premiere; February 11, 1954
Filming took place sporadically from 1940 until the end of the war, originally on location in Spain and then, because of wartime currency restrictions, at a village set constructed in Mittenwald, Bavaria. At the end of the war, French occupation authorities impounded the footage and Riefenstahl did not regain possession until the early 1950s.

DIE ROTEN TEUFEL (THE RED DEVILS)—unrealized film
Production companies: Leni Riefenstahl-Produktion and Junta-Film
Director: Leni Riefenstahl
Script: Leni Riefenstahl, Joachim Bartsch, and Harald Reinl
Camera: Bruno Mondi, Walter Frentz, Guzzi Lantschner, Otto Lantschner
Cast: Vittorio de Sica, Brigitte Bardot, and others
Die Roten Teufel advanced further than most of Riefenstahl's unrealized film projects. A shooting script was in hand and the cast contracted when political controversy prompted financial backers to withdraw from the project.

Mid-1950's

DIE EWIGE GIPFEL (THE ETERNAL SUMMIT)—unrealized film
Meant to be filmed as a documentary with five chapters, each concerning the climbing of a major summit in a different part of the world.

DIE DREI STERNE AM MANTEL DER MADONNA (THE THREE STARS ON THE CLOAK OF THE MADONNA)—unrealized film
Intended as a vehicle for Italian actress Anna Magnani who ultimately rejected the role.

TÄNZER VON FLORENZ (THE DANCER OF FLORENCE)—unrealized film

Written only in treatment form, it chronicled the life of the famous dancer Harald Kreuzberg, with whom Riefenstahl had performed as a young dancer in Berlin.

FRIEDRICH UND VOLTAIRE (FREDERICK THE GREAT AND VOLTAIRE)—unrealized film
A collaboration with French film director Jean Cocteau; the two gathered historical material and anecdotes, but Cocteau's bad health and financing problems doomed the project.

1956

SCHWARZE FRACHT (BLACK CARGO)—unrealized film
Production company: Sternfilm GmbH
Director: Leni Riefenstahl
Script: Leni Riefenstahl, after the book of the same name by Hans Otto Meissner
Camera: Heinz Hölscher, R. von Theumer
Visualized as a mixture of feature film and documentary about the slave traffic still flourishing from eastern Africa into Arabia, the outbreak of the Suez War halted preliminary shooting. Other difficulties plagued the project, from a near-fatal accident for Riefenstahl while searching for locations to rainy seasons. Finally, the project lost its financial support.

1960

THE BLUE LIGHT—unrealized film
In 1960, the English production company Adventure Ltd. approached Riefenstahl about a remake of *The Blue Light,* envisioned as a ballet-fairy tale filmed in color. Riefenstahl collaborated on a new script, but the project proceeded no further.

1970's to present

DIE NUBA (THE NUBAS)—unfinished film
A documentary of the Nuba tribes of the Sudan; Riefenstahl and

camera assistant Horst Kettner shot footage along with Riefenstahl's still photos, later published in several internationally acclaimed books. According to Riefenstahl's memoirs, the footage remains unedited in her Munich editing rooms, with completion unlikely due to her age and health.

BIBLIOGRAPHY

Books

Barkhausen, Hans; Coultass, Clive; Geyrhofer, Friedrich; Jagschitz, Gerhard; Priessnitz, Reinhard; Reimers, Karl Friedrich; and Siegert, Michael. *Propaganda und Gegenpropaganda im Film 1933–1945.* Vienna: Austrian Filmmuseum, 1972.

Becker, Wolfgang. *Film und Herrschaft: Organisationsprinzipien und Organisationsstrukturen der nationalsozialistischen Filmpropaganda.* Berlin: Verlag Volker Spiess, 1973.

Breker, Arno. *Im Strahlungsfeld der Ereignisse.* Preussisch Oldendorf, Germany: Verlag K. W. Shuetz, 1972.

Bucher, Felix. *Screen Series: Germany.* New York: A. S. Barnes, 1970.

Burden, Hamilton T. *The Nuremberg Party Rallies: 1923–39.* New York: Frederick A. Praeger, 1967.

Cadars, Pierre and Courtade, Francis. *Geschichte des Films im Dritten Reich.* Munich: Carl Hanser Verlag, 1975.

Denzer, Kurt. "Untersuchungen zur Filmdramaturgie des Dritten Reiches." Unpublished doctoral dissertation, the Christian Albrechts University of Kiel, Germany, 1970.

Eisner, Lotte. *The Haunted Screen: Expressionism in the German Cinema and the Influence of Max Reinhardt.* Berkeley and Los Angeles: University of California Press, 1969.

Fanck, Dr. Arnold. *Er Fuehrte Regie mit Gletschern, Stuermen, und Lawinen.* Munich: Nymphenburger Verlagshandlung, 1973.

163

Graham, Cooper C. *Leni Riefenstahl and Olympia*. Metuchen, NJ: Scarecrow Press, 1986.

Grunberger, Richard. *The 12 Year Reich: A Social History of Nazi Germany 1933–1945*. New York: Ballantine Books, 1971.

Hull, David Stewart. *Film in the Third Reich*. Berkeley and Los Angeles: University of California Press, 1969.

Jaeger, Ernst. *Leni Riefenstahl's Olympia Film*. Berlin: Olympia Film G.m.b.H., 1938.

Kalbus, Dr. Oskar. *Vom Werden Deutscher Filmkunst: Der Tonfilm*. Altona, Germany: Cigaretten Bilderdienst, 1935.

Kracauer, Siegfried. *From Caligari to Hitler: A Psychological Study of the German Film*. Princeton, NJ: Princeton University Press, 1947.

Leiser, Erwin. *Deutschland Erwache! Propaganda im Film des Dritten Reiches*. Hamburg: Rowohlt Taschenbuch Verlag, 1968.

Manvell, Roger and Fraenkel, Heinrich. *The German Cinema*. New York: Praeger Publishers, 1971.

Riefenstahl, Leni. *Hinter den Kulissen des Reichsparteitagfilms*. Munich: Franz Eher Verlag, 1935.

———. *Kampf in Schnee und Eis*. Leipzig: Hesse & Becker Verlag, 1933.

———. *The Last of the Nuba*. New York: Harper and Row, 1973.

———. *Leni Riefenstahl Memoiren*. Munich: Albrecht Knaus Verlag, 1987.

———. *Schoenheit im Olympischen Kampf*. Berlin: Deutschen Verlag, 1937.

Shirer, William L. *Berlin Diary*. New York: Popular Library, 1940.

———. *The Rise and Fall of the Third Reich*. New York: Simon and Schuster, 1959.

Speer, Albert. *Inside the Third Reich.* New York: The Macmillan Company, 1970.

Trenker, Luis. *Das Grosse Luis Trenker Buch.* Munich: C. Bertelsmann Verlag, 1974.

Wollenberg, H. H. *Fifty Years of German Film.* London: The Falcon Press Limited, 1948.

Wykes, Alan. *The Nuremberg Rallies.* New York: Ballantine Books, 1970.

Zeman, Z. A. B. *Nazi Propaganda.* Oxford: Oxford University Press, 1964.

Articles

Alpert, Hollis. "The Lively Ghost of Leni." *Saturday Review,* March 25, 1972, pp. 65–67.

Barkhausen, Hans. "Footnote to the History of Riefenstahl's *Olympia.*" *Film Quarterly* (Fall 1974), 8–12.

———. "War auch Walter Ruttmann Politisch Blind?" Unpublished article in the collection of the Deutsches Institut für Filmkunde in Wiesbaden.

Barsam, Richard. "Leni Riefenstahl: Artifice and Truth in a World Apart." *Film Comment* (November-December 1973), 32–37.

"Biographical Sketch of Leni Riefenstahl." *Film Comment,* III (Winter 1965), 12–15.

Brownlow, Kevin. "Leni Riefenstahl." *Film* (Winter 1966), 14–19.

Brownlow, Kevin and Riefenstahl, Leni. "A Reply to Paul Rotha." *Film* (Spring 1967), 14–15.

Corliss, Richard. "Leni Riefenstahl: A Bibliography." *Film Heritage* (Fall 1969), 27–36.

"Das Blaue Licht: Urauffuehrung im Ufa-Palast am Zoo," *Berlin Morgenpost,* April 1932.

Delahaye, Michel. "Leni and the Wolf: Interview with Leni Riefenstahl." *Cahiers du Cinema in English,* No. 5, 49–55.

"Filmografie." *Filmkritik* (August 1972), 435–41.

Gardner, Robert. "Can the Will Triumph?" *Film Comment,* III (Winter 1965), 28–31.

Gregor, Ulrich. "A Comeback for Leni Riefenstahl?" *Film Comment,* III (Winter 1965), 24–25.

Gunston, David. "Leni Riefenstahl." *Film Quarterly* (Fall 1960), 5–19.

"Henry Jaworsky Interviewed by Gordon Hitchens, Kirk Bond, and John Hanhardt." *Film Culture* (Spring 1973), 122–167.

Hinton, David B. and Sontag, Susan. "An Exchange on Leni Riefenstahl." *The New York Review of Books,* September 18, 1975, pp. 58–60.

Hitchens, Gordon. "An Interview with a Legend." *Film Comment,* III (Winter 1965), 4–10.

"Jean Cocteau's Letters to Leni Riefenstahl." *Film Culture* (Spring 1973), 90–93.

Kelman, Ken. "Propaganda as Vision—Triumph of the Will." *Film Culture* (Spring 1973), 168–171.

Lambert, Gavin. "Nazi Cinema." *Films and Filming* (August 1975), 48–49.

"Leni Riefenstahl Interviewed by Gordon Hitchens." *Film Culture* (Spring 1973), 94–121.

"Leni's 'Rote Teufel'—Ein Gespraech mit Frau Riefenstahl." *Hamburger Abendblatt,* April 25, 1953.

Lewis, Marshall. "Triumph of the Will: Program Notes." *Film Comment,* III (Winter 1965), 22–23.

McLemore, Henry. "Propaganda? Not in This Film!" *Hollywood News-Citizen,* December 16, 1938.

Manilla, James. "A Review of a Lesser Riefenstahl Work." *Film Comment,* III (Winter 1965), 23.

Mannheim, L. Andrew. "Leni." *Modern Photography,* February 1974, pp. 88–119.

Marcorelles, Louis. "The Nazi Cinema." *Sight and Sound* (Autumn 1955), 65–69.

"Misguided Genius." *Newsweek,* September 16, 1974, p. 61.

"Mussolini Total fur den Olympia Film: Deutschlands Triumph auf der Biennale," *Neues Wiener Journal,* September 2, 1938.

"Nazi Critical Praise for Olympia." *Film Culture* (Spring 1973), 196–197.

"Nazi Critical Praise for Triumph of the Will." *Film Culture* (Spring 1973), 174–175.

"Olympiad 1936–Andrew Sarris and Dick Schaap Discuss the Riefenstahl Film." *Film Culture* (Spring 1973), 181–193.

"Olympiad (XI) Thrilling Record of Great Games." *Los Angeles Times,* December 17, 1938.

"Production Credits for Olympia." *Film Culture* (Spring 1973), 194–195.

"Production Credits for Triumph of the Will." *Film Culture* (Spring 1973), 172–173.

Riefenstahl, Leni *"Notizen zu Penthesilea."* *Filmkritik* (August 1972), 416–425.

———. "The Production of the Olympia Films: Incorrect Statements and Their Refutation." *Film Culture* (Spring 1973), 176–180.

———. "Why I Am Filming Penthesilea." *Film Culture* (Spring 1973), 198–222.

Rotha, Paul. "I Deplore. . . ." *Film* (Spring 1967), 12–14.

Schulberg, Budd. "Nazi Pin-Up Girl." *The Saturday Evening Post,*
March 30, 1946, pp. 11–41.

Sontag, Susan. "Fascinating Fascism." *The New York Review of Books,*
February 6, 1975, pp. 23–28.

"The Rise and Fall of Leni Riefenstahl." *Oui,* May 1973, pp.
73–106.

"This Future is Entirely Ours: The Sound and Picture Outline for
Leni Riefenstahl's Triumph of the Will." *Film Comment,* III
(Winter 1965), 16–22.

"Tiefland." Buehnenblaetter fur die 195. Spielzeit 1973/74, Na-
tionaltheater Mannheim.

Vogel, Amos. "Can We Now Forget the Evil That She Did?" *The
New York Times,* May 13, 1973.

Weigel, Herman. "Interview mit Leni Riefenstahl." *Filmkritik*
(August 1972), 395–410.

————. "Randbemerkungen zum Thema." *Filmkritik,* (August
1972), 426–433.

Weiss, Trude. "The Blue Light." *Close Up* (June 1932), pp.
119–123.

INDEX